DWIGHT YORKE

DWIGHT YORKE

by Hunter Davies

First published in 1999
by Manchester United Books
an imprint of André Deutsch Ltd
76 Dean Street
London W1V 5HA

www.vci.co.uk

A catalogue record for this book is available from the British Library

ISBN 0 233 99759 8

1 3 5 7 9 10 8 6 4 2

Jacket design by Button
Plate section design by Design 23
Typeset by Derek Doyle & Associates, Liverpool
Printed and bound by
Butler and Tanner, Frome and London

Contents

Foreword

A minor warning. This book is not all about football. Anoraks looking for football facts and figures might be disappointed. In fact there are only three matches in the book. Modern Manchester United fans can guess which ones.

I go to football all the time, watching Spurs, my team, and also Arsenal, another local team, as well as about 100 live matches a season on television. Though I love football dearly and write about it constantly, matches fade so quickly from my mind I have to concentrate hard to remember scores from last week, never mind individual moves. When asked for my all-time favourite goal, as anoraks do, my memory goes blank.

I also can't take in reports of football matches, unless I have seen them and am reading about them the very next morning, so they are still relatively fresh. When they turn up in books years later, blow-by-blow accounts of past performances, even ones where I was present, I start skipping. So I have spared myself, and you, what I consider the boredom of long dead games.

Football is the background here. The foreground is the life of a person from the West Indies who has ended up playing for one of the best-known football clubs in the world. Or at least in search of his life, for I have been equally interested and concerned with the people who helped and guided him or were just there, along the way.

It's a book I've been waiting to write for over 25 years. In that time I have done four football books – a novel, a World Cup book, a collection of football pieces, a year in the life of a football team – but not a biography. People have been mentioned and I've thought, hmm, far too young, what can they have to say.

Gary Lineker was suggested and I tried to think of what to ask him that I didn't know the answers to already. Then about three months later I woke up with an idea of how to do it.

In anyone's life, but particularly with sports people, there are always people better, bigger, faster, thought more likely to succeed at every stage. At primary school, playing for the Under 14s, in your town or area, there's bound to be a player rated above you. Even when you do make it to a professional club and become a youth player, no one knows which one or two out of the 20 or so youths will make it in the end. What then happens to those who didn't? And what do they think of the person who did? I would find them and filter them in, between chapters.

So I rang the publisher and said I had a great idea for Lineker's biography. Too late, he said someone else is doing it.

I have hugged this format for a few years, waiting for someone to walk into it. Then two things happened. Over the last three years I have been working on a travel book about the West Indies, during which I have visited 27 different islands. To amuse myself in Guadeloupe I tried to find the village where Thierry Henry's family came from. As we know, a great many of the French World Cup winning team had Caribbean or African antecedents. In Tobago, I kept on meeting people who said they had sat next to Dwight Yorke at school. About half the island said that. Must have been big classes.

Then, by chance, I was invited to lunch by a football agent, Jonathan Holmes, whom I have known for years, who wanted me to meet a new partner of his, Tony Stephens. He turned out to be Dwight Yorke's agent, among many others'. Out of that lunch, came the idea for the book.

The attraction of Dwight was not just that he was a star

player, and had just moved to a star club, but his age. The notion of a book about a 27-year-old might seem preposterous in the general field of biographies. I have written eight biographies: from writers, engineers to pop stars – most of them long dead, apart from the pop stars, who were very living at the time.

In popular music, as in football, the stars are young, and the superstars often have biographies written of them. I seem to have seen biogs of Kevin Keegan coming out for as long as I have followed football. Young Michael Owen, at the age of 19, is currently contracted for not one but three books, though only one is biographical.

In football terms, at 27, Dwight Yorke is a senior prefect, if not a senior citizen, likely to have seen most things, ups and downs. On my first meeting with him, I checked I had not missed a book about him, perhaps done locally in Birmingham, or even in Tobago. Nothing, he said, though he had had offers. 'I only want to do a book when I have achieved something.'

The trouble, for a biographer, writing about someone in the maelstrom of achievements, as Dwight turned out to be, is getting them to sit still, to concentrate on the questions, to look back, to think, to take time, when their whole world and his agent is after them. I had the same problem with the Beatles. You have the fun of observing young people at their peak, or what you suspect could possibly be their peak, but to them it is their normal, frantic life which they expect always to go on. They are not really concerned, at that time, with pinning it down, recording it, analysing it, just with living it. I like to think that, in 20 years' time, Dwight will look back and be pleased to see that I tracked down so many people from his life and got their memories.

I also like to think the book is as much social history as sport. Perhaps the biggest attraction of all was the fact that he had come from a different culture, seeing us, as an outsider, and also giving us glimpses of his own background. So there is a lot about the lives and problems of people in Tobago. And also about the lives and problems of English football coaches, managers, agents and even football landladies.

I have also not forgotten the others, along the way. In Tobago and England, I have tried my best to describe what happened to them.

But what happened to Dwight, how he got from there to here, that's the main story, the big match.

Hunter Davies, Loweswater, August 1999

Introduction

The twenty-sixth of May 1999 would have been Sir Matt Busby's 90th birthday, if he had lived. Which he does, in a way, to Manchester United supporters, in their myths and legends. Just as the 13 players who took part in that game that night will live on, in legends and myths, despite what might happen to them in their future temporal lives.

The Bayern Munich team was sure no shock was coming. How could it, after what had gone before? They had been 1–0 ahead in the final of the European Champions League for 85 minutes of the game – from the fifth minute to the 90th. During that time, they had hit the woodwork twice from two of the few flowing movements of the game. Manchester United had not created one clear-cut chance, nor forced the Bayern goalkeeper into a half-decent save. Bayern had played well, defended stoutly, no panics, no mistakes. Dammit, they deserved to win. One even gave a triumphant gesture to the fans.

No need to be a Bayern fan or player to feel it was in the bag. The 500 million watching round the world could also sense it was all over. It had been a fairly boring, pedestrian game for the uncommitted, many of whom had already gone to the lavatory, put the kettle on, or just switched off.

Usually in football, and in life, there are hints and signs, suggestions which don't necessarily lead to resolutions, but there had been nothing at all to indicate that Manchester United could do it. And now we were into the 90th minute.

Then out of nowhere came those two scrambled, totally unexpected goals. In a theatrical drama, it's called *deus ex machina*. When God, or similar, somewhere out there, decides to fiddle with the scenery and the scenario.

Afterwards, none of the participants could move their bodies, see out of their eyes, look into their minds, understand what had happened. Bayern had not been beaten by a better team on the night, nor by better play. That would have been some consolation, some explanation. Beaten by, well, by what? It must have been God. As one German newspaper announced next day, 'God is an Englishman'. If it didn't prove there was a God, it did prove that Life is not fair, Life is not predictable.

'Football, bloody hell,' said Alex Ferguson afterwards. How wise. Spoken from experience.

Manchester United's supporters felt the same. Yes, they had done it before, coming back from one down to Spurs in the final league game of the season to win the Premier League. Coming back from two down against Juventus in an earlier round of the European Cup. But even they had not come back from what in football is death, that moment when the 90-minute mark is up. Now they had done it, and won the Treble.

Next day, the nation viewed this unexpected victory as proof that the English never-say-die spirit was not dead. Manchester United, the most loved and also the most hated club team in England had been metamorphosed into a national team, waving the banner for the entire country. Tony Banks, then Minister of Sport, saw it as a sign that yes, the nation would now get to hold the 2006 World Cup. His rationale was not quite clear, but if he believed it, then no one cared about logic at such an emotional time.

On BBC Radio Four's *Today* programme, the 'Thought for

the Day' religious message was based on Manchester United's famous victory. Time Can Stand Still, the speaker said, the Last Minute Matters, You CAN Repent, Even at the Moment of Death. Or words to that effect.

Thirteen Manchester United players took away their own morals and tales to tell their grandchildren. For one of them, Dwight Yorke, it was his first experience of winning something on this scale. He had joined Manchester United only that season. Now he had won three major honours in ten days, the third before a crowd of 90,000 in Barcelona. That was about double the population of the tiny island whence he had come, an island and country not known for producing footballers. He'd had an evening on a world stage, which as a player playing for his own small country is unlikely ever to happen to him. He had scored more goals that season than anyone else in the Premiership. He had been voted Player of the Season by the football managers.

Two months later, the manager was knighted by the Queen, which was thought only fair and just by a grateful nation. The Queen, on conferring the honour, showed her deep and meaningful knowledge of football by suggesting that the Treble would not be won again. Sir Alex, as a good citizen, agreed.

'The Queen was right,' said Sir Alex. 'The culmination of three trophies was the pinnacle of my career.'

Meanwhile Dwight went home, to become a legend in his own little island.

Part 1
TOBAGO

1

My first memory is of almost being killed. This was when I was about two years old. It's not an actual memory. Just what I've been told. You'll have to ask my mother. It's become a family story, a story that was often told to me. Who knows now which bits are true or not.

I was out in the street one day, at home in Tobago, in the village of Canaan, where we lived. It's a busy street, near the airport. I was going somewhere or other with one of my brothers.

Across the road I suddenly saw one of my sisters. I think she was in a shop and she waved at me through a window. So I ran across the road to her. A car hit me and carried me on its bonnet for about 100 yards. I suppose I must have been knocked unconscious. Yeah. Must have been. As I say, I can't remember it all. I was too young.

Then this Chinese guy got out of a car behind, not the one who'd hit me, but from another car. He turned out to be a doctor. He treated me and gave me some sort of injection. No, not got a clue what sort of injection. It's just what I've been told. No one ever found out his name, from that day to this. I don't know why. That's all I know.

My mother thought it was divine intervention, that there was some guardian angel looking after me. I still think that, basically. That I'm being looked after in life ...

3

I was the eighth of nine children. My mother Grace used to be a hotel cleaner, at Crown Reef Hotel, near where we lived. It's still a hotel, but has been rebuilt as a luxury model, the Coco Reef. My father was a dustman. He's still working for the council, I think, but is now head of it, or head of something. I'm not quite sure. He's called Fulton Yorke and he came from the village of Buccoo, just up the coast from where we lived.

I've got three sisters and five brothers. Juliet is the oldest and I think she must be about 44 by now. I was born in 1971, then Brent came two years later in 1973. There was about a two-year age difference between us all.

We lived in a two-bedroom bungalow. When I was little, I shared a bed with Brent, in the same bedroom as my mum and dad. I suppose I must have done. That's my memory. The other seven must have shared the other bedroom, at some stage, I suppose. But as they all got older, some of them left and there was more room.

I can clearly remember not liking sharing the bed with Brent. He'd go to bed earlier than me, being younger. Once when I got in with him the bed was wet. I turned the mattress over or round and tried to find a dry bit. Oh, he can't deny it, I can remember it only too well.

We were poor and sometimes there wasn't enough food to go round, with having so many mouths to feed, and so many school fees to pay. Yeah, you're right, you don't pay for education in the West Indies, that's true, but all parents have to pay for the uniforms. You have to wear uniform at every school. And pay for books and stuff. So with nine kids, it was expensive.

But we didn't starve. In the Caribbean you can always find something to eat – mangoes or you'd climb a palm tree and get a coconut and drink the juice and eat the jelly. You'd always find something to eat to keep yourself alive, but sometimes you'd much prefer a hot meal.

If there was nothing to eat at home, I'd go round the neighbours and see if they had anything. I was a nice polite kid. So I usually got something.

The first school I went to was an infants school – Baby Jo's. I don't know who or what she was. She was a woman, probably called Jo, and she took in babies while mothers went out working. I was nervous about going, but I don't remember crying. Just nervous.

Then at five I went to Bon Accord Primary school. I remember the sports teacher there, Kenny Crooks. He was a big influence on me.

From about the age of six, all I lived for was sport. That was when I suppose I first realised I was good at games. It's just luck, really, having that sort of skill. I did everything – cricket, marathon running, basketball, netball – but I loved football best. I was always small for my age, but I had stocky thighs. No, I don't know where my basic skill came from. Not my dad, because he was crap at football or sports – which he'll probably deny. I think I got it from my mother. She was good at netball when she was at school. My bigger brothers were always pretty good, especially Clint, who was ten years older than me. He was very good at cricket.

I didn't do much school work. I don't think I was useless. I'd have been sort of average, if I'd put my mind to it, which I didn't.

My best friend at school was Rama. No, that's not his real name. In Tobago, everyone has a nickname, and you never know where it's come from, but it goes with them through life. He's still a good friend. I often think that if I hadn't made it in football, I'd be Rama today. No, he doesn't do much. Bit of this and that, getting by. I stay in contact with him and see him when I'm in Tobago. I know that if he had turned out to be me, he would have stayed in contact.

I used to go crabbing with Rama, to get some money. Everyone in Tobago loves crabs. It's a big thing. Crab bake, that's very good. Not on the beach, but in the bush. The crabs lived in holes and you'd find the hole and lay a trap, a home-made wooden trap. You'd bait it with something, a bit of cheese or something. Then you'd sit and wait for it to come out. When it rained, that was a good time for catching crabs, that's when they usually all came out.

We'd sell the crabs for $24 a dozen (TT dollars) to restaurants, shops or to neighbours. Crab and dumpling, that's another big dish in Tobago.

Yeah, I do have some quite happy memories of my early childhood, even though we were so poor. I know my mother had a lot of struggle, a lot to put up with. She was the dominant one in the house. I don't remember much about my father ...

Tobago is a paradise island. Small, bijou, neatly formed, with some picture-postcard white-sandy, palm-treed beaches, tropical vegetation, aquamarine coral reefs. Should you be on holiday in the West Indies, it's one of the nicest, prettiest places to visit, with some of the nicest, pleasantest people.

Some islands, such as Anguilla and the Bahamas, are so flat they can become monotonous, despite the perfect beaches. Some are so hilly, so rocky, such as Saba, so densely forested like Dominica, that they are tough to get into, to travel around in, so they remain largely undeveloped. Tobago is blessed with a variety of landscape.

The southern tip, where the airport is situated, and where most visitors arrive, is flat and well developed, easy to zip across. The lush rolling hills and rain forests are in the middle and to the north, with waterfalls, rivers, magnificent trees and exotic birds. The rain forest, now a national park, is the oldest, legally protected forest in the world. Yet none of the hilly bits or forested bits is too high or impenetrable.

Tobago likes to refer to itself as 'Robinson Crusoe's Island' for reasons never quite clear, except it does look like the sort of tropical island Defoe's hero might well have been stranded on. It is also sometimes called Treasure

Island, suggesting it was the inspiration for Robert Louis Stevenson's story, a claim made by several other Caribbean islands, all of them spurious. R.L.S. never went to the West Indies. The map of Treasure Island came out of his head. But you get the picture. Tobago is a pretty, pretty place.

Quite small, just 27 miles long by eight miles or so across, with a population of 50,000. The capital is Scarborough, to the south of the island, on the Atlantic coast. It is unusual for a Caribbean island to have its capital on the rougher, Atlantic side. Usually they plump for the smoother, velvety calm Caribbean coast. It's a rather dusty little town, with an unattractive harbour, but once you climb out of Scarborough itself, up to the old Fort King George, then it's stunning scenery, all the way.

Right along the Caribbean coast are some beautiful beaches. My favourite is Englishman's Bay, totally natural and unspoiled, curving in an arc, palm-fringed, with rocks at either end, as if framed by God to show off its beauty. I've stayed on 27 different Caribbean islands, so far, and Englishman's Bay is always the one I see best and clearest in my mind's eye.

The bay's name is a clue to Tobago's colonial past. But there are also many place names with French-sounding connections – such as Buccoo, where Dwight's father came from, or Bon Accord school which Dwight attended. Other place names hint of past battles and dramas, such as Bloody Bay and Man O' War Bay. Like almost all Caribbean islands, Tobago was fought over for many centuries by assorted European nations, killing each other for political power, or for control of the sugar plantations which were worked by imported African slaves.

Tobago ended up English speaking, belonging to Britain from 1814. They have of course their own accent and dialect, as do all parts of the English-speaking globe, though often so-called proper English-speaking

Englishers are confused by what they hear. 'Is English we speaking,' so Tobagonians reply. In England, Dwight is referred to as a Tobagan. In Tobago, they call themselves Tobagonians, a word which took me six months to get my tongue round.

In 1888, Tobago was joined to Trinidad as a single unit, inside our glorious Empire on which the sun hardly ever set. Since 1962, it has been independent, but still joined to Trinidad. There have been recent murmurings about going it alone, but most Tobagonians seem happy to be citizens of Trinidad and Tobago.

Trinidad, 21 miles away, is decidedly different. Not just much bigger in size and population, with 1.25 million people, but different in its history and development. It's industrial for a start, most unusual for the Caribbean, thanks to the discovery of oil and the development of assorted petroleum products. It's also ethnically very mixed. Some 40 per cent are of Indian origin, 40 per cent African, with the rest being European or Chinese.

In Tobago, by comparison, almost all are of black African origin. There are no visible signs of any leftover white plantocracy, which you get in Barbados and Jamaica, usually still hanging on to a lot of the land and money. Tobago's plantation owners and managers, even in the old days, were absentee owners. The moneyed classes tended to live on Trinidad, though they might have a holiday home in Tobago.

Tobagonians, especially the older ones, see Trinidad as the wicked island, beset with crime and drugs, violence and noise, much of which, alas, is fairly true, but at the same time, Trinidad is exciting, dynamic, vibrant, with a thriving cultural and artistic life. Trinidadians see Tobago as the sticks, rural and backward, the way Londoners might view the Hebrides. They consider Tobagonians friendly enough, but dozy and simple, even a bit stupid. A pretty island, more restful than Trinidad, but not much has ever come out of

Tobago, so they think, either artists, calypso musicians or sporting heroes.

As in all Caribbean islands with long-standing British connections, such as Barbados and Jamaica, sporting heroes can become very big heroes, with airports and boulevards named after them. By sport we mean of course cricket or athletics, two areas in which West Indians have traditionally shone.

Dwight Yorke, growing up poor in little Tobago, knew nothing and experienced little of the natural wonders and beauty of his own island. Canaan, the village where he was born, is right in the south of the island, almost at the airport, a dusty, scrubby, low-lying area, far from the rain forest and those unspoiled, empty beaches.

There is one noted beauty spot nearby, Pigeon Point. A little peninsula of white sand with excellent swimming, turquoise water, a pretty little pier, changing rooms and a beach bar. But not for the likes of Dwight or his family. You have to pay, then and now, for entrance to Pigeon Point. A nominal sum, but always beyond the likes of the Yorke family.

Grace, his mother, was born Grace Joseph in 1939 in Scarborough, but grew up in Canaan. She had eight sisters and four brothers. Their father was a shoemaker and she went to Bon Accord Moravian school, though they were brought up Anglican. At 14 she started work at the nearby Crown Reef hotel. She was in the laundry for a while, then the kitchens, earning TT$188 (about £18 today) a week. She says it never went up, in the five years she worked there.

She met Fulton Yorke through sewing. She wanted to learn, hoping to earn more money. He at the time was working at a tailor's. They got married at St Patrick's Anglican church in 1961.

'When we first married,' she says, 'we lived with my grandmother for about three years. Then she give we a piece of land, and we built a house upon it. It was a National Housing scheme. The Government built it, and we paid for it. We paid TT$25 a week and after 25 years, we own it.'

It was just a simple concrete and breeze-block house, two bedrooms and a living room with a little porch at the front but quite a bit of garden behind. The kitchen was outside, a 'dirt earth kitchen,' so Grace called it. There was no bathroom or lavatory for the simple reason that they had no water. That had to be fetched from a stand-by tap at the end of the road. The road, in those days, was still a dirt track, with no pavements. It didn't have a name.

Grace was bigger and heftier than I expected. No reason, really, except that Dwight was always small for his age, and today can still look quite frail on the pitch when faced by giant defenders. Fulton was even more of a surprise when I first caught sight of him. He is large, burly and imposing, 6ft 3in tall with a trim moustache, handsome if rather fiercesome.

He was born in Patience Hill in 1938. His father, Joseph Yorke, was a fisherman and his mother, Mary Magdalen Guy, was a housewife.

'I went to a Roman Catholic school, even though we were Anglicans. I left school at 14 and became an apprentice tailor. I did that for eight years, making pants and jackets. No salary. I never got paid. I was just an apprentice. To make any money, I gathered coconuts.

'In 1957, I joined the Department of Works, digging the roads, labouring to the masons. Sometimes I was laid off and had no work and no money. Then I worked on the Mount Irvine golf course, building the bunkers and the fairways.

'As a feller, I always loved music. I'm a steel band man. I play the pans. I still do. Bass pans. While I was working at Mount Irvine, I got the owner, an Englishman, to sponsor our steel band. That's why we call ourselves the Mount Irvine Buccaneers. I will spell it for you ...'

What about your time as a dustman?

'I is coming to that. We haven't reached that point yet. Then I went to Trinidad for a time, looking for work. I worked with T Clay products, as a labourer, then I came back to Tobago.

'I got married to Grace on 26 August 1961. I had seen her as little boy, long before we started courting.'

It took me some time, and some problems before I got that information out of Fulton.

'Juliet was my first, born on 24 September 1955,' said Grace. 'Her name come from the old people. My grandmother, she gave her the name Juliet.

'Verlaine came next, born on 7 April 1958.'

That sounded French, perhaps after the French poet, Paul Verlaine. It could be a remnant of Tobago's French connections. Grace didn't know anything about that. And anyway Verlaine is a girl.

'I just loved the name Verlaine. Someone in the village was already called Verlaine.

'Keith was my first boy, born 25 March 1960, then came Clint on 7 June 1962. Both lovely names. That's why I chose them.

'Deborah was born on 9 January 1964 and Gary on 10 January 1966. Verlaine,' she suddenly shouted. 'Was Gary 10 January ...?'

I hadn't realised till then that Verlaine was inside the house. She was also quite big, taller than her mother. She came out onto the porch and confirmed Gary's birthday was 10 January. Grace said that was the only one she ever got wrong, confusing it with Fulton's, whose birthway is 8 January.

'Dwight was born on 3 November 1971, and Brent on 18 September 1973.'

Naturally, I asked where the name Dwight had come

from. Was that just another lovely name?

'I sitting here, just before he was nearly being born, and past the gate I saw this fat, chubby boy going to school. He was called Dwight Moore, aged about ten. I think he looks so nice, so happy, if I have a boy, I'll call him Dwight.'

'He was born here, in this house. With some I went to the hospital, if I could get any transport. Let me think. Five were born here. Four in hospital. Dwight came so quickly I couldn't have made it to the hospital anyway. He was nine pounds, I think. Round about that.'

Was he a good baby? 'They all good babies.'

The fateful day of the accident, which Grace can remember only too well, was 28 July 1974. So Dwight was right about his age – just two and a half years old.

'I had sent Clint and Dwight off to church with some bread I had baked and some paw paw cake. They had delivered it, and were on the way home, when it happened.'

Clint, aged 12, was holding Dwight by the hand, walking along Milford Road, the main road, dead straight for about four miles, which leads from the airport towards Scarborough.

Across the road was Verlaine, aged 16, with Garth, aged six. When Dwight caught sight of his big sister, he pulled his hand away from Clint's and dashed over. Straight into the path of a car.

Verlaine remembers it as being about 6.30 in the evening. Dusk was descending, as it does in the summer months. In the winter, the sun sets about 6.00. She estimates the car was doing about 60 mph.

Dwight bounced off the front bumper, then was run over by the car. The undercarriage did not touch him, nor fortunately did the wheels, but the car's red-hot exhaust burned a swathe of skin across his back.

'All I saw was Dwight bouncing,' says Garth.

'All I could hear was the gnashing of brakes,' says Clint.

'All I did was bawl,' says Verlaine. 'I just stood there,

bawling. But I did recognise the driver of the car. It was a man who lived not far away from us. He did stop, and I screamed at him. He said he thought it was a stray child, and that it wasn't his fault. Then he drove away.'

'Two things saved Dwight,' says Clint. 'One, he was quite small, so the car ran right over him, except for the exhaust. And two, the Chinaman who got out from another car and attended to him.'

Verlaine is the source of the Chinaman story. Though, on cross examination, she said he might have been a white man. Anyway, he was definitely a stranger, probably a tourist, hurrying to catch a plane.

'We didn't know Dwight had been hit by the exhaust,' says Verlaine, 'till we tore off his jersey. Then we saw the burn marks. He was just lying there, unconscious.'

News of the crash, and the body of a child lying on the main road, spread immediately. Grace, sitting at home, just two streets away, was soon told.

'A neighbour came shouting down the street – Dwight's dead! I rushed to the main road, just in time to go with him to the hospital. Another car had stopped and took him to Scarborough.

'He was in hospital three months. He had a broken leg and bad burns. He was very happy in hospital. The staff loved him and made a fuss of him. He was always a jolly little feller, even when he had been run over.'

The accident was never reported to the police. No insurance or injury claim was made. The driver of the vehicle is now dead. But the accident lives on in the Yorke family legend – as does the scar.

'It's strange,' says Grace, 'but it didn't seem so big at first, when he came out of hospital. But it got bigger as he got bigger.'

'Even stranger,' says Garth, 'is its shape. It's turned into the map of Tobago.'

'My mother and my grandmother,' says Clint, 'both

believed that God had saved Dwight for a purpose. And every year that has gone by since then, we can see what the purpose was ...'

From about the age of eight, my ambition was to be a professional footballer. I remember thinking that when I am, I'll look after my mother, because she's been so good to me.

I didn't know anyone from Tobago who had ever become a professional player. Or how you became one. Or anything.

I played all the time, from morning till night. With my brothers and sisters, or anyone. As I got a bit older, and found I could play quite well, I always wanted to play with the bigger kids.

Mostly we didn't have a football. I'd kick any old thing around. Anything. Coconuts. Fruit. If I had a football, I went to bed with it, then I'd wake up with a football beside me and start playing again.

When I was about eight, a football coaching clinic had been recently opened in Scarborough by Bertille St Clair. He asked me to join. I don't know how he knew about me. I suppose he'd gone round the villages, asked who was good, or he'd watched kids playing in the streets.

The trouble was that his clinic was on Saturday mornings – from 9.00. My mother is a Seventh Day Adventist. That's how I was brought up. Adventist services are on Saturday mornings – at 9.00. So my Mum, as head of the family, was very upset when I wanted to go. She said I had to go to church. I wanted to do the right thing by her, but at the same time I wanted to have the football coaching.

I had such an urge to play football, even when I was only a little kid. I can't remember not having it.

Sometimes, early on, my mum would refuse to let me go, saying I had to go to church today. But most Saturdays I managed it.

The other problem was getting there. I couldn't afford the bus fare, unless I'd managed to sell some crabs. Mostly I had to hitch-

hike, get a lift with someone I knew, or stand in the main road and hope a stranger would stop.

You did have to pay for the coaching clinic. Not much. About 20 local dollars a season. I think that's what it was. I can't remember how I always managed to get it, but I did.

I was the sort of smiley, cheerful kid who could always get the odd dollar out of people. I always said 'good morning' to people in the street and was polite. That was how my mother had brought me up. That's how I got fed, begging it from people, when there was no food in the house.

We did have one or two bad guys living near us. Not really drug dealers, well, not exactly, but you know, people who were thought to be the local bad guys. I got on well with them. When I had no money I'd go and ask them for a dollar to catch the bus to Scarborough for the coaching clinic.

Lots of little kids would go and ask them for money, all the time. Usually they'd just waste it. They knew with me I was spending it on something good, getting the bus to coaching. They knew I would value it. They admired me in a way, I suppose, even though I was just a little kid.

I had no football boots, or any football kit. I went in my shoes, my only shoes, which I used for school. So that didn't please my mother.

The coaching took place on a grass pitch, but we had no goals, just two sticks, and no lines. There were always arguments when the ball was thought to have gone out.

We were split into groups according to age – 8–10-year-olds, 10–12, 14–16. When you got into the top group you were the top boys. We called them the pros.

I loved every moment of it. It was just so fascinating, to be told what to do, how to improve. I listened to every word Bertille told me and practised everything at home on my own.

My friends were always older boys, because I was soon playing in teams with older kids. There were two older boys I hero worshipped. One was Russell Latapy, who was about three years older than me. Everyone looked up to him. We called him the Little Magician.

The other was Wendell Moore. He really was my role model. He was so respected, so highly regarded – and very polite. I based myself on him. I wanted to be him. He was in Bertille St Clair's coaching clinic, but he was about three years older than me. It was a big day when I got to carry his bags.

Wendell played for Tobago school boys and I remember going to see him play against a Trinidad school team in what we called the Intercol Cup. This was a competition between all the Secondary Schools in Trinidad and Tobago. Trinidad is so much bigger than Tobago, so you didn't have the Tobago team playing the whole of Trinidad. Tobago was just one of the groups that the country as a whole was split into: North, South, Central, West or whatever. Wendell played well, when I watched him, but Tobago that year didn't get to the final.

There were several others with great ability. Oh yeah, more than me. No question. I don't know why they didn't go on and capitalise on their abilities. I suppose I was lucky. Or perhaps it was because they didn't want to succeed enough. The way I did.

I did think of nothing else. I played all the time, even inside the house, if my mother was out. I was once kicking a ball in the house when I broke the television – a black-and-white set, which my father had just bought. When he came home he was furious. I was in bed asleep by then, but he woke me up and hit me. No, he wasn't brutal. I wouldn't say that about him.

Once we had that television, I always used to watch the football. We got what was called Big League Soccer – which was always an English top side. I think we got the match live. I don't know. I wasn't aware of it not being live or being recorded, but I know we did see whole games.

I liked Liverpool, but my favourite team was Spurs. I loved Hoddle and Waddle and Ardiles. Especially Hoddle. Most of all Hoddle. He was my professional hero.

Football coaching would finish at 11.00 on Saturday mornings, then I'd rush home to watch Spurs at 12.00.

I watched Hoddle most of all, watching his every movement,

trying to copy all his tricks, all the little things he did. My only desire in life was to be like Hoddle ...

4 Grace Yorke, Dwight's mother, had said she was born an Anglican, and got married in an Anglican church. So what happened?

'I changed,' she explained. 'And Dwight was the first of my children to be offered up. That's what we call it, when you join the Adventist church.

'Anyone who knows the Bible knows the Ten Commandments. We all know not to steal, not to commit adultery, we know all those sorts of sins, but people forget the Tenth Commandment – to keep the Seventh Day Holy. Everyone should keep the Seventh Day Holy. So that's why I became an Adventist.'

But don't all Christian churches keep Sundays holy?

'Not Sundays. Saturdays. Don't you know that Saturday is the seventh day of the week?'

Er, not really.

'Well it's in the Bible. You should read it. Sunday is the first day of the week, so Saturday is the seventh.'

Back to football. Was she really upset when Dwight chose to go to football coaching rather than church?

'Well, Mr St Clair was a very respected man, so I trusted him. And I knew how much Dwight loved football.

'The only thing that worried me, when he started all this football, was hanging around with bigger boys. I didn't like that. Dwight was always sensible, but I thought the big boys would be a bad influence.

'It was all he thought about. He would do his jobs, his household chores, but he'd rush them, and the minute my back was turned, he was out, playing football. Even if he was just kicking a calabash around.'

A calabash? I thought that was a tree. Surely Mr St Clair didn't suggest that kicking trees was good training? That's for the likes of Tommy Smith and Graeme Souness, heroes that Dwight once had, till he moved on to worshipping the more delicate skills of the Blessed Hoddle.

Mrs Yorke then shouted for Gary to go and get me a calabash. There used to be a tree right in front of their house, she said, when Dwight was young, but it had been cut down. There was another, not far away.

Inside the house, I could see Gary slumped in front of the television, lying on the floor, watching cricket. He was clearly not all that keen to go off and get me a calabash. His mother shouted to him again, so off he went. He came back with one, then was told to clean it.

When it was cleaned, she gave it to me, saying I must take the 'bowlie' back to England. That was what they always called it.

It did look remarkably like a football, almost perfectly round, like a light-weight, circular coconut, grey in colour, the colour which old footballs made of leather always used to go, once they had been kicked around. I gave it a little kick. It was quite light, being hollow inside, but brittle. You might easily break your toe on it, if your feet were bare and you were only eight years old.

'One of the things he loved was playing in the rain. They would play outside, in the rain and the mud. No, they didn't mess the house. They got washed under the tap, outside.'

Deborah, his sister, often played with them, usually as goalie. Deborah, her mother says, was very good at all sports.

'She played in goal with no top on. She had no breasts at the time. I suppose she must have been about fourteen. Dwight would be seven. This is before he started the coaching lessons.'

One of the things often forgotten about the West Indies is the rain. You just have to observe the lush vegetation to be aware of it. Often a downpour will last only 40 seconds, and can be most refreshing, but in the so-called rainy season – from July to December – it can last all day and be torrential. The rainy season is also the football season in Tobago. It's then too wet for playing the real national game – cricket.

It meant that growing up, Dwight might not have boots or balls, but he always had grass to play on. A decided advantage. Growing up in most African countries, you are very unlikely ever to play on grass. Even so-called proper pitches, with goals and lines and nets, are on hard grit or dirty sand. In 1990, I went to write about football in the Cameroon, one of the surprise teams of the World Cup in Italy. The thing which surprised me most was the fact that in the whole country, only two pitches had grass.

Dwight also had the advantage of sporting brothers and sisters who liked to play all games, all the time. At his little coaching classes, Dwight had his football heroes, like Wendell Moore, even though there seemed little chance of them getting very far as footballers. But at home he saw his big brother Clint, ten years older, soon starting to do really well as a cricketer. Clint got into the Tobago cricket team as a school boy, and then the national team.

I expected Clint to look much like Dwight, or the two other brothers I'd already met, Garth and Gary, both of whom are much the same size and build as Dwight. Clint turned out to be 6ft 2in tall and well built, more like his father.

Clint thinks he might have been helped to grow big by having to do one of the domestic chores when he was growing up. 'My job was to fetch the water. There was a tap at either end of our street, each about a 100 yards away. I had to fetch all the water for the house, twice a day. That made me strong.'

Another job was looking after Dwight, taking care of him when he was out, such as on the day of the accident. Which was of course not Clint's fault.

'I had a lot of responsibility for Dwight when he was little. My Mum was always telling me to look after him, especially when he was hanging out with bigger boys. He was always very small, so he did stand out when he was with them. It was funny, watching him play with them. When he was aged about six, he'd play with boys twice as old. They'd kick him about, kick him down, but he'd just get up and smile. The only time he ever cried was when they said to him no, you can't play with us, you too small.'

Everyone, in and outside the family, speaks of Dwight's constant cheerfulness, politeness, good humour, which naturally endeared him to everyone.

'He never disobedient,' says Grace. 'Anything you axe him to do, he do. Give him a hundred things, and he do them, but very quickly, so he play soccer. I never see him vexed.'

What about the smiley face? Known now to all English football fans. Where did that come from?

Grace's own natural expression, watching her sitting on her front porch, seemed, how shall I put this, more towards the worried than the cheerful. As for Fulton, in my brief glimpse of him so far, he appeared to scowl rather than smile.

Grace thought hard. Yes, she said, the Yorkes on the whole did not have naturally smiley faces. Only two of her children were born with a natural smile – Dwight and his sister Deborah. The rest, well, they were just normal.

'Dwight, when he was little, looked so nice and cheerful that we know him as Anna. That was the nickname we give him.'

Why?

'Because he look like a girl.'

Grace made a sideways mock grimacing face, knowing I would tell Dwight this. Which I looked forward to.

In Tobago, as a whole, there is a natural tendency to break into a smile, given half or even the smallest chance. They can look worried at first, but as soon as something is said which is in any way faintly amusing, their faces, their whole bodies, will burst into life, rocking with laughter.

They are also extremely courteous towards strangers,

trusting, unsuspicious, un-grasping, un-hustling. This, alas, cannot be said about all West Indian islands today, though on the whole, the smaller ones tend to have the friendliest people.

Then the poverty of the Yorke family. How true or typical was that?

'Yes, sometimes we had no food at home,' says Grace.

'As they got bigger, I went back to work, doing sewing or crochet, leaving Verlaine to look after the little ones.

'One August I did fetching water for the road men. I did that for ten days and got TT$500. That was a lot.

'I needed money for food and also their clothes. I made pants for all the boys, but as they got bigger, they didn't like wearing them. "Why she make pants for me. I too big for she pant." That's what they always say to me.'

Grace smiled at this, a Dwight-type smile, spreading over her face.

Apart from sewing and stitching to help her family, she also grew vegetables in her back garden – cassava, potatoes and dasheen – for them to eat.

I presumed that when Dwight caught one of his famous crabs he would give one to his mum for the family pot.

'Oh no. We don't eat crab.'

Why not?

'Adventists don't. It's in the Bible. We don't eat pork and we don't eat fish without scales, so that includes crab. Dwight get those crabs to sell, to make him pocket change. Do you say pocket change in England?'

I finally, and carefully, got round to asking about the big, handsome Fulton, wondering what part he played in bringing up and caring for his nine children.

'He never at home,' said Grace quietly.

So what did you do for money?

'He give me sometimes.'

When Dwight had spoken about him, I could sense him choosing his words with care. His father did get mentioned, such as the time he broke the TV, but very rarely. And when he did, there was never ever any criticism. Perhaps, of course, he was not aware of what was happening. Just took it as normal.

All the brothers talk constantly about their mother, when remembering their childhood, not their father, who would appear to have been absent a lot. Their mother, for example, was the one who punished them. What sort of punishment, I asked Garth.

'I'm not sure I should tell you this,' he said. 'But she was the one who gave us licks.'

Such as?

'Well, she used to make us get down on each knee and we'd have to hold a big stone in each hand. If we'd been really naughty, we'd have to stay like that for 20 minutes. That was the worst punishment.'

Didn't sound too bad. Fulton, being big and strong, might have hurt much more, if he had been there more often. So where was he? Away in Trinidad, perhaps, looking for work?

I asked one family friend about Fulton, not long after I had arrived in Canaan.

'He likes swimming.'

That's what I thought he replied, so I made a swimming motion, to show I'd understood.

'No, he likes wimmin ...'

So that was it. Not at all untypical in the West Indies, then or now. Or many countries, come to that.

When I was eight I was selected for trials for the Trinidad and Tobago Under 12s team. The trials were in zones at first, then I was picked for the full trial. I was still aged eight, as far as I remember.

I then went on to play for the national schoolboy

team. When I got to ten, I was in the Under 14s, then at 14, I was in the Under 16s.

One of the boys I played with in the Under 12s and the Under 14s national team was Brian Lara. He became one of my best friends. He's from Trinidad, not Tobago, but we got on well. He played midfield, and was excellent. He could have made it as a player, I'm sure, but he was even better at cricket.

I did my first foreign trip when I was about ten. We went to Costa Rica for a schoolboy tournament. I was joint top scorer, but we didn't reach the final.

I travelled a lot with the national schoolboy teams, all round the Caribbean. I also went to the States. We played in Miami and in Colorado Springs. But I was still going to Bertille's coaching clinic. He had his own team as well, which I played for.

I practised skills all the time at home – teaching myself to use my left foot, as Bertille said a real footballer has to do that.

I was still small at 13, just about 5ft I suppose, but Bertille trained me to be tougher and stronger. I didn't play striker, but usually wide on the right.

One day when I was about 13 or so, Bertille caught me in the street with some of my street friends. I don't know what he was doing in our street. He just suddenly appeared.

I was drinking a Carib beer with some other boys. Just hanging around the block, liming, as we call it in the West Indies.

Bertille went mad when he saw me. He rushed across and shouted at me. He said I would never make a footballer. Not now. That was it. Not unless I kept my body fit and healthy.

He then ordered me to do press-ups in the street. There and then, in front of my friends. It was terrible. I felt he was just want-ing to really show me up in front of my friends. They were all embarrassed for me as they watched me doing the press-ups.

Yeah, I suppose I could have walked away, just ignored Bertille. But I did the press-ups, as he told me.

That was the sort of kid I was. I basically wanted to do well, to do what I was told.

I never had another drink from that day till I was 21. And I've *never smoked or taken drugs. I believed what Bertille said. To make it as a pro footballer, you had to be fit and healthy, in mind and body ...*

6 Bertille St Clair is a legendary figure in Tobagonian football. Everyone knows him, everyone recognises him. He's very easy to spot because he is so amazingly insignificant. Small, thin, weedy and bespectacled. Not at all physically terrifying, but you can tell at once from his demeanour that he is not someone to be messed around with. He looks a bit like Chalkie, the teacher with the skull-like head who used to appear in cartoons by Giles, the archetypal demon little teacher who was used to scaring generations of schoolchildren, big and small.

Dwight, even now, doesn't seem to know much about him, what he did in real life, or how he appeared in Dwight's own life. Just that he did appear – and everything then changed. And Dwight has been grateful ever since. A career which had existed only in his mind, based on pure fantasy, became a possibility when Bertille came along. Well, a maybe, might-be, half-fantasy sort of possibility. After all, no one knew anyone who had gone that way before.

In a normal, football-playing, football-structured country, it is hard for anyone with recognisable talent not to be spotted at some stage, to be recommended to a scout, to have a trial of some sort, with some sort of professional club. But in a small, isolated, West Indian island, with no professional football league, no system of scouting, no tradition of producing footballers, the chances were always against it. No wonder that Dwight still believes he would have ended like Rama, his crab-catching friend, if Bertille had not come along.

Bertille was born in 1942 at Black Rock in Tobago. He was one of six children, the son of a truck driver. I asked about his name, unusual, not to say rather poncy, for a Toboganian. He agrees there might be some French influence somewhere, or perhaps from his father, who came originally from Grenada.

He went to Scarborough Boys' School and started teaching at 16. He was unqualified at that stage, but at that time there was still in Tobago the old Victorian method of senior pupils teaching younger ones. Eventually, through in-service courses and some time at college, he became a trained teacher.

As a boy, he had played a lot of football, but just for a local club. At 16 he broke his leg, rather nastily, which never properly healed. I had noticed his rather unsteady gait from afar, and thought perhaps he might have developed arthritis, being no longer a young man, but he said no, it was the residue of his injury. He pulled up his trousers to let me see. The injury had left him with one leg twisted and shorter than the other, so his walk has always been awkward.

A common story, then, of someone keen on football, whose own career is brought to a premature end, who decides to devote himself to the flowering of others.

While school teaching, he found himself in charge of all school games – netball for girls as well as cricket and football for boys – but football was his first love.

Inside primary schools, it is always a matter of chance to find a master truly interested in football. But outside, there was no system in Tobago at the time for coaching or encouraging those interested in improving their football skills.

'I began my coaching school in 1976, just with 20 guys. I hired Shaw Park from 9.00 to 11.00 on Saturday mornings.'

Shaw Park, in Scarborough, is Tobago's 'national' stadium. That's how the locals see it, but it's on a level with a municipal park pitch, for Sunday-morning players, with no proper facilities. Dwight, according to his memories, said they didn't even have goals, but Bertille says they did, for the bigger boys at least.

'In 1978, I went on a coaching course in Mexico, to get

myself qualified as a football coach. I went on another in 1980.'

So when Dwight came along in 1980, aged eight, Bertille's coaching clinic had grown to about 50 kids and he himself had become properly qualified.

In the early years, he was still on the lookout for likely lads, and would ask around the villages for any names, though very soon there was a waiting list, and he no longer needed to go out searching.

'I think someone did tell me about Dwight, someone who had seen him playing in the street or on a bit of waste ground. So I approached him, told him and his mother, about my coaching clinic. The fee in 1980 was only TT$5 [about 50p] a month. As I knew Dwight couldn't afford that, I let him in for free, if he arrived with no money.

'I was impressed from the beginning, not just by his natural skills but his determination to learn and improve.'

When the call came for Dwight to have trials at national level for the Under 12s team, there was then the problem of getting himself across to Trinidad. This had always been an obstacle for likely kids from Tobago, especially from a poor family, with an unsupportive and sometimes missing father. It's one thing to be invited to a trial. Another thing to get there, across the ocean, when you are only eight years old.

'I met him once at Tobago airport,' says Selwyn Archer, a neighbour in his 50s, who was aware of the family background.

'It was very early in the morning and I was going to Trinidad for the day to watch the horse racing. I was surprised to see Dwight there, aged about eight or nine, I suppose. He looked totally lost. He said there was supposed to be a message and ticket for him, but he couldn't find it and didn't know what to do. He had to be at this place in Trinidad, something called Augustine. He wasn't sure of the name and didn't know where it was.

'I bought a ticket for him and took him with me on the

plane. The place turned out to be St Augustus school. I took him there, gave him TT\$40, and said I would return for him.

'I didn't come back from the racing till midday. The place seemed deserted and I couldn't see him at first. Then I found him and Colvin Hutchinson asleep on a bench.

'Another time I took him with me to Trinidad as a treat to watch Flamingo of Brazil play a friendly match against Trinidad. All the way through, Dwight kept on jumping up and pointing at this player, saying that's the one I want to be like, that's the player I want to be. It was Zico. He didn't know Zico's name of course.

'Dwight was also very good at cricket, but I could see his heart was set on football. I told him he should concentrate on football, and give up cricket.

'When he got to the final trial for the national Under 12s team, I had a whip-round in the village, asking for contributions to get him there, pay his expenses. I only got TT\$5.

'When he got in the team, to go and play in Puerto Rico, I offered to give him TT\$20 for every goal he scored. Mr Bull Cowie, a friend of mine in the village, said he would do the same, give Dwight TT\$20 for every goal.'

Note that this game was in Puerto Rico – not Costa Rica as Dwight remembered. But then he was very young.

It was not a one-off match but a knock-out competition being held in Puerto Rico between eight Caribbean and American countries – Puerto Rico, the Dominican Republic, the Dutch West Indies, Mexico, Haiti, the USA and Trinidad and Tobago. It took place in San Juan between 13 and 18 July 1981. So Dwight was in fact nine and a half years old.

Bertille St Clair remembers the dates exactly, and got out the faded newspaper cuttings to show me. He was at the time the newly appointed coach for the Under 12s. Another bit of luck, in that he already knew about Dwight and had made sure he was called to all the trials.

'A lot of people said he too young and too small to get into the team, but I knew how good he was. I said he had to play.

'We did have one problem with him in the hotel. With another boy, Russel Latapy, he was playing in the elevator. They somehow jammed it and Dwight damaged his hand.

'He had to go and see a doctor as his hand was so bad. I remember the doctor who treated Dwight thought he was wonderful. Fell in love with him. Said he wanted to adopt him.

'I told Dwight off for playing in the elevator. I said that's it. He had been disobedient in the hotel, and now would not be in the next game. He started crying and pleading with me.

'I was of course going to play him anyway, as I knew how good he was. He was only a child. He'd never seen a lift before.

'I remember when he scored his first goal we were in this proper stadium, which had a flashing score board. Whenever someone scored, it started flashing GOAL! GOAL! GOAL! Dwight had never seen one before. When he scored, he just stood there, staring at it. The game restarted – and he was still standing there, staring at the screen. I had to jump up and shout at him to take up his position.

'We were beaten in the final by the USA, but Dwight scored most goals in the competition.'

Bertille clearly remembers the incident with Dwight drinking a bottle of Carib beer. He says it took place after the return from that Puerto Rico tournament – so Dwight was only nine and a half, not 13, as he remembered. And Bertille had not appeared in the street just by chance.

'I knew that they would be celebrating in his village, as Dwight had been the star goal scorer. It was in the Trinidad newspapers. So that evening I went to his village to see he was OK, that none of the big boys were leading him astray.

'So I was mad when I saw him with a bottle of beer in his mouth. I realised it had been given to him by some of the big boys and that he wasn't really a beer drinker, but I knew where that could lead. So I got out of my car and rushed across and slapped him.'

You slapped him?

'Of course I did. Round his face. I just slapped Dwight. Not the big boys. I wouldn't have hit them. Then I made him do the press-ups in front of me.'

It is interesting that Dwight had said nothing about being hit by Bertille. Corporal punishment, administered by school teachers upon pupils, is of course common in Tobago, then and now. The incident clearly made a big impression on Dwight, but perhaps it was being hit in front of his friends that had really embarrassed him, not just the press-ups. The slap had not been mentioned, possibly to spare Bertille's embarrassment today.

Selwyn Archer, the friendly neighbour, paid up his bet, giving Dwight the dollars for scoring all the goals. But Mr Bull Cowie never did. He said he didn't have the money. He had already given Clint, Dwight's brother, a present of two mango trees for having scored so many runs for Trinidad and Tobago. He went and took back the two trees – and gave them to Dwight instead.

So that was good, then.

You can see why I didn't do so well at school, with playing so much football, travelling so much. I was quite good at maths, I liked doing maths, but I didn't do any work.

Naturally, I failed the Common Entrance exam, our sort of 11-plus. In my class of 33, I should think only about ten passed it. I then went to Scarborough High School, when I was about 12. At 14, I went on to Signal Hill Comprehensive.

At 14, I stopped living at home and went to live with my friend Sherwin Patrick. He was the goalie in our school team. No, he wasn't better off than us, he just had more space in his house. I was always staying at his house and he was my friend, so I just moved into his home and shared a bunk with him.

When I was 15, I got into the Under 19s national team. We had a pretty good team, so that was exciting.

Then the World Cup qualifications were getting started. We had a good national team and it looked as if they might qualify for Italy 1990. That was even more exciting. Trinidad and Tobago had never got that far before. We were in the Concacaf region. I'm not sure what the letters stand for, but it covers the Caribbean countries and North America. That was our region, for World Cup qualification, but only one team from that region would go through to Italy.

I was on the fringes of the national team, training with them. I was always having to travel to Trinidad, for training and matches, and it became more and more awkward living in Tobago, especially when things were getting so important for the national team.

One day Jack Warner, who was President of our FA, came to our house and said to my mother that it would be better if I lived in Trinidad. He said it would be hard to keep up my input, if I stayed in Tobago.

I didn't want to leave Tobago. And I think my mother wasn't keen. Then there was the problem of my education, as I was still at school. But I realised I had to make sacrifices, if I wanted to succeed.

So at the age of 15, I moved to Trinidad. I lived with Jack Warner, in his house, with his family. I went to school in Trinidad, at a place called Arouca.

Lots of arrangements were made for me, about transferring schools. I didn't really understand what was going on, but I think even the Prime Minister got involved.

They were doing everything, you see, to help the national team do well. So anyone who seemed likely to play for them, they got helped as well.

When I came to sit my GCSEs, I was playing a match, or train-

ing, and couldn't sit them, so it was arranged for me to sit them later, on my own.

I eventually got into the national team when I was 16, and still at school. We did well, and were soon getting near the top of our group.

We all began to think that we really would make it to Italy. You can't believe how excited everyone was, in a little country like ours, where football had never been the national game. Cricket had always been much bigger. But now we were doing well at football, which surprised everyone.

It was very good timing for me. So you have to say I was lucky, coming through when I did. Compared with say Wendell Moore and the others from Tobago before me. They were good boys, but they were three years or more older than me. Most of them by now had left school and got some work, doing ordinary jobs, given up hopes of a football career.

I got all this encouragement because, for the first time ever, football was so big. They wanted to have their best squad possible, give them the best training and give them the best chance. Every time we won a match, we got treated like superstars. Everyone knew our names. Doors opened everywhere. It was amazing, coming from a little island like Tobago. It was like suddenly being treated as royalty.

8 While star pupils move on, school teachers stay put, polishing their memories and, with a bit of luck, polishing the cups and medals which their former pupils won for their school teams, all those years ago.

Kenny Crooks was the teacher in charge of sports at Bon Accord Government School which Dwight attended from the age of five till 11. He comes from Canaan, and still lives there, with his wife and four children. He remembers the road accident when Dwight got injured. It happened almost outside his front door, and the news went round the neighbourhood, though he wasn't at home at the time.

He picked Dwight for both the cricket and football school teams from about the age of nine, which was very young, considering the school, then and now, had pupils up to the age of 15. He still has photos of the school teams, in 1981 and 1982, showing Dwight looking incredibly young and small. His brother Garth, three years older, was also in the same school team.

Mr Crooks also taught maths in the school and says that Dwight definitely had talent. 'There was no problem he couldn't have solved. He could have been outstanding at maths, but of course he didn't do any work.'

Hard to estimate the truth of this. School teachers can look back with rose-coloured specs, just like anyone else. When Dwight says that but for football, he would have ended up like Rama, with no real job, I suspect this is an exaggeration the other way. Someone with the will and discipline to succeed in football would presumably have put his mind to getting a decent job, if just as an accounts clerk in an office or at the airport. Most people at Canaan seem to work at the airport. I had noticed that Dwight does have a good head for telephone numbers, having memorised scores of them, but then, when not playing or training, he does spend his life on the phone.

'But as a footballer,' continued Mr Crooks, 'Dwight really was exceptional at every stage. That doesn't often happen. Usually other boys catch up with them, and they fall behind. Wendell Moore did equally well before him. He was also at our school. He was an excellent player. You have to be, coming from Tobago. I always think you have to be two or three times better than people in Trinidad to make it into a national team. They get the exposure and the help we don't.

'We had a very good team when Dwight was here – partly due to him. We won the national championships for primary schools. No, not just in Tobago, but in the whole of Trinidad and Tobago. We then went on to win it seven years in a row.'

Bon Accord Government School was the biggest primary in Tobago, but competing against the city slicker schools from Port of Spain in Trinidad, that was a much bigger challenge.

Dwight stayed on for a while, when he failed his Common Entrance, becoming what is called 'post primary', the ones who stay on till fifteen, taking no exams, going into ordinary jobs, if of course they can get any work at all.

The brain boxes in Tobago who fly through the Common Entrance go on to the Bishop's High School, the *crème de la crème*, which usually means the sons and daughters of those with a more middle-class background or aspirations. They do exist, even in a small island such as Tobago, people like white-collar workers, government officials, teachers, lawyers, doctors, some of them of course able to use tutors, for that extra bit of coaching. Bishop's is in effect a grammar school – the only one on the island. Then and now, Tobagonians feel deprived educationally, complaining that they have not enough secondary school places for their children.

But there were also two other secondary schools, not quite as élitist or academic as Bishop's, but perfectly good, for which you still had to pass the Common Entrance. Which Dwight did not. It was thanks to Mr Crooks and other teachers that Dwight was able to move on to Scarborough High.

'It was the first time it had happened,' says Orville London who was then vice principal at Scarborough High. He is from Tobago, but unlike Bertille, he is a graduate teacher, taking a degree in sociology and history at the University of the West Indies in Trinidad. He later became Principal of Signal Hill, the next school Dwight attended.

'We decided to award him a scholarship. Not a money scholarship, but a place at the school, because of his exceptional ability at football. He had played for national teams, so it was clear he had not been able to concentrate on his school studies. I discussed it with Mr Warne, who was Principal of Scarborough High at the time, and Mr Crooks at Bon Accord. We all approved of letting Dwight in without having passed the appropriate exams.

'Other educators might not agree, but I have always been of the opinion that outside interests should be factored in to a pupil's progress. They should get credit for succeeding at outside activities, whatever they are, not just the academic. By accepting Dwight, it sent signals to others that they too should try hard.

'We broke the rules for Dwight, but afterwards did it quite a few times, for pupils who had done well at sports.'

The advantage to Dwight was that he got a secondary education, even if he was still giving most of his attention to football. He also got better exposure as a footballer. By attending a secondary school, Dwight could play in the national and Intercol league, against secondary schools from all over Trinidad. Something he could not have done at Bon Accord primary.

The advantage to Scarborough High and Signal Hill was that they got a star player for their teams. So their action was not totally altruistic.

In the autumn of 1987, Signal Hill achieved a great victory over their local rivals, the poshos of Bishop's High, beating them 4–0 to win the Tobago zone of the Intercol cup.

'In yet another series of scintillating performances in the Park,' so the *Tobago News* reported, 'Yorke almost single-handedly orchestrated the Bishop's humiliation. In the fifth minute, he dribbled around two defenders and slipped the ball past another, for Calvin Hutchinson to slam home.

Signal Hill in Intercol playoffs

"THIS Anna is tears," commented one ebullient schoolmate as he left Shaw Park after Signal Hill Senior Comprehensive's 4-nil victory over Bishop's High School in the Tobago zone Intercol final last Sunday.

And local fans are confident that if Dwight "Anna" Yorke maintains last Sunday's form, he could lead Signal Hill into next Saturday's national final.

In yet another in a series of scintillating performances in the Park, Yorke almost singlehandedly orchestrated the Bishop's humiliation.

In the 5th minute, he dribbled around two defenders and slipped the ball past another for Calvin Hutchinson to slam home.

Then in the 27th he drifted down the left side, split the defence with a perfect pass and Gary Solomon climaxed the move.

In the second half, it was Sean John who was at the end of a right side cross in the 49th minute and then 20 minutes later, Yorke did it all himself, outrunning the defence and insolently nudging past an advancing goalkeeper.

But in spite of this comfortable victory, the courageous Bishop's outfit was able to highlight if not exploit some weaknesses in the Signal Hill line up.

The right wing back seemed suspicious, vulnerable; Calvin Hitchinson, although no where near his best form and the clinical efficiency which will be so essential when the opposition is tougher and chances are fewer.

And these are problems which will have to be solved if Signal Hill is to justify the growing confidence of their supporters go on to win both the National Intercol league titles this year.

'Local fans are confident that if Dwight "Anna" Yorke maintains last Sunday's form, he could lead Signal Hill into next Saturday's national final.'

Note that Dwight's nickname of Anna was being generally used at this time. Also a minor misprint: it should have been Colvin not Calvin Hutchinson.

Signal Hill did go on to win the national final, the *Tobago News* – which had first appeared only two years previously, in 1985 – cleared the pages for a photo spread and full reports in their edition of 7 November 1987.

'Dwight was the most talented all-round sportsman we ever had,' says Orville London. 'He was good at cross country, table tennis, everything. I remember him taking up badminton and in two weeks he was able to beat people who had played for years. He did end up *victor ludorum* of the school.

'There came a time when he could have been overwhelmed by the nature of his football success, carried away by being a national player. I did have to pull him in line, now and then.'

35

In what way?

'Well I did flog him, once or twice. Not on the hands. We used a rod on the bottom.

'I can't remember exactly what he'd done. Shows it can't have been very serious. Minor insolence, probably, rather than anything preposterous or outrageous. I had hundreds of pupils after Dwight, so it's hard to remember details.

'By being a star player at 12 or 13, he found people wanting to be his friend. Yes, and I'm thinking of girls, girls much older, girls aged 14 or 15. Now that is a temptation, that is a danger, when girls of 15 or so are after you, are interested in you. On the whole, I think he coped with that situation. It didn't get out of hand. He was always well mannered, mild mannered, polite. It's a great tribute to his strength of character.'

Mr London was personally more interested in cricket than football, being President of the Tobago Cricket Board – eventually going on to the heights of the West Indian Cricket Board. But he had to admit that Dwight was best at football.

'All the same, I didn't see what he was really capable of. I thought his zenith would be playing for Trinidad and Tobago. It was the likes of Bertille St Clair and others who had the vision. They were determined that his talents should not be confined to the national team. And they didn't just see this vision. They didn't just talk the talk. They worked the work ...'

Bertille certainly had great faith in Dwight, but he also had equal faith in Wendell Moore.

'Dwight was always an inspirational player,' says Bertille.

'We could see the potential, but when he was 16, I have to admit that I thought Wendell was the better player for his age. I had such high hopes for Wendell.

'When Wendell was just over 16, he got a trial with Bristol Rovers. Bobby Gould was the manager. I'd got in touch with him through a friend of friends, different contacts. To pay for his trip, we held school dances, organised events, to raise money to send him to Bristol. He went for the trial – but it never led to anything. Which was a shame. But I think in a way it spurred Dwight on to even greater efforts.

'Every Saturday morning, in my coaching clinic, I used to say to the boys, "One of you will HAVE to make it." After all the work we had done, all the talent I knew we had, eventually one of them would get through and become a proper professional. If of course they worked hard.

'One of my sayings is that there are no elevators in football. There are no short cuts, no lifts to take you up. You have to climb there, step by step.

'"Put your feet in another man's boots." That's another of my sayings. By that I mean do unto others as you want to be done by. Don't kick, don't cheat, stick to the rules, be disciplined.

'I left Dwight out of a team once, because he was late turning up. It was hard to do, as he was the best player. But I had to – to teach him lessons. I suppose I did become a father figure to him. I used to bring back as many boys in my car as I could, when we'd been playing in villages in the north of the island. Some of them, like Dwight, I would stick in the boot. Dwight of course was always quite small.

'I did meet his father Fulton once. He said to me, "He's your son, do what you like with him, do what you can ..."'

In 1989, Aston Villa football team came on a tour of Trinidad and Tobago, playing friendly matches. I don't know why they came. Perhaps a pre-season tour. I've no idea how it came about, or whether this was a normal sort of thing. I just heard they were going to play us.

It was great for us, to play against a proper professional club. We wanted to reach the World Cup finals, so the more matches against better teams the better.

They played us first in Trinidad, against the whole national team. It was a huge event and we played in the National Stadium. They beat us 1–0.

Next day, Villa played against a Tobago 11 – and I found myself travelling back to Tobago on the same plane with them. I was playing for Tobago as well.

It was a massive game for Tobago. We just didn't see these sorts of players in Tobago. In fact I don't think it had happened before. Having a professional team playing in Tobago.

There were about 4,000 people in the Shaw Stadium. Usually it was just a handful.

They were much better than us and were soon easily ahead. At half time, their manager Graham Taylor asked if I would come on Villa's side, and play the second half for them. It was just to see how I got on, playing with professional players.

I wanted to, of course, but the rest of our team didn't. Somehow the crowd and everyone else found out and started complaining. To Villa, it was just a little harmless friendly, but for Tobago it was a big thing. So how could I play for the opposition? Why should they have our best player? That's what everyone was shouting. So I stayed on the Tobago side. We got beaten 5–0.

But because of that game, Graham Taylor said he would like to give me a trial.

Would I come to Birmingham and spend a few weeks training with Villa? That's what I was told. Then they would be able to decide whether I might make it or not as a professional player.

I left all the arrangements for travelling to Birmingham to my manager Neil Wilson. Well, that's what I called him. He was vaguely looking after my affairs.

All I cared about was getting a trial with a proper team, something I had dreamed about for years ...

Dwight was just 17½ when the Call came, so his life had not been very long so far, but he'd first had the fantasy of being a footballer when he was eight years old. So, for most of his life, he'd had that dream.

In many ways, he was a late starter, when you think of the likes of say, well to pick a name at random, David Beckham. At the age of 11, young David was playing at Old Trafford. Not quite a professional, prodigious though his talent was, but he had won the London area of a competition for young players, organised by Bobby Charlton's Soccer Coaching School. He then went on to win the final in Manchester. Sir Bobby himself said he was the best 11-year-old he had seen in six years of running the school. Could a young person with such a fantasy life ask for more? Lucky beggar.

David Beckham, though not by any means from a wealthy family, also had incredibly supportive parents, including a father who drove him everywhere, did everything for him, almost subjugated his own life to him, in order to make sure he had the best of starts in his football life, from buying him the best boots to securing him the best exposure and advice.

Yet Dwight, at 17½, so he says, had acquired a manager. How could that have happened, when he was an amateur, earning nothing, playing for nobody? His club, the one which Bertille St Clair ran, was more of a boys' club than a football club.

I couldn't find Neil Wilson's home phone number in the Tobago telephone book. I'd been told he worked at the airport, but I was given different numbers for different days, so I decided to doorstep him at his home on a Sunday.

In Tobago, being such a small island, everyone knows where almost everyone else lives, even if they don't know the address, especially if they have the smallest position in the local community or economy.

So I asked a taxi driver outside my hotel – the same Coral Reef where Grace Yorke used to work – to take me to Neil Wilson's house. No problem, he said, he knew it well. When we got there, I told him to wait, in case I got the bum's rush. Lots of big dogs and a suspicious security officer at the gate. I explained my purpose and the security guard looked even more suspicious. This was the judge's house, he said. What did I want with him?

Neil Wilson's was further up the hill. A handsome, bungalow-style house, with big windows, lots of satellite antennae, and a security gate but no guard or intercom. I shouted over the gate and eventually a youth wandered out, listened to my request, and went off.

Neil Wilson himself came to let me in – aged 65, thin, moustache, rather distinguished, very friendly, very helpful. He was and still is one of Tobago's leading businessmen. He had a travel agency and a jewellery shop, though today he mostly works at the airport as the local manager for Caledonian Airways, and Liat and Condor, the German package-holiday airline, owned by Lufthansa.

'I first heard about Dwight in 1983, when he was 12 years old. Bertille came to my office one day to say he was looking for some sponsorship for a young Tobagonian boy. He'd got in the national Under 14s team to play abroad, I think it was in El Salvador, but had no money, no funds, no family to give him pocket money. I said where is he then. Bertille then brought him in. He was this little guy, very small, but with a very big head. "Can he play?" I said to Bertille. '"He's a whiz," Bertille replied. 'So I took out my wallet and gave him US$50. That was his pocket money for the tournament. I had helped other local youngsters over the years, in various ways, but what I remember about Dwight was that he brought me back a present from El Salvador. Or it might have been

Honduras. Anyway, he bought it out of my money. It was only a postcard, but an expensive, laminated one. It was the fact that he'd bothered, that he'd remembered. Boys don't always do that. Not that I was helping him in order to be thanked.'

So why were you? Was it to get your name or firm mentioned somewhere as a sponsor?

'No. There was nothing at all in it for me. I just felt sorry for him. I remember once in my car, when I was driving him somewhere, we passed a house and Dwight said, "That's the house where a lady friend of my father lives." I felt so sorry that he didn't have the normal sort of fatherly encouragement. I knew his mother was poor, that they often didn't have food on the table. Yet he was such a nice little guy.

'As he got older, he was always at this house. My son used to drive him to school. When he passed his driving test, he didn't of course have a car, but I let him drive mine.

'I remember him sitting there, where you are sitting, one evening with a girlfriend. He must have been about 16. I asked him what he wanted to do with his life. "Manage," he said. Yes, he called me manager, or manage for short. "All I want to be is a professional footballer." I promised him there and then I would help him to get a professional contract.

'I had no interest in football at the time, knew nothing about football contracts. The first time I saw Dwight play was in the Intercol Cup for Signal Hill, when they beat St Benedict from Trinidad. He was outstanding. He always seemed small in real life, but on the pitch, he was about ten feet high.

'I went to see his mother, when I decided to help him with his career, and she was a bit worried. "You taking my son away," she says. "He always by you ..." '

Mr Wilson was putting on Grace's voice at this stage, a thicker West Indian accent than Mr Wilson's own, though not by very much. 'By you' Grace meant being with Mr Wilson, at his house, most of the time.

DWIGHT YORKE

REPUBLIC OF TRINIDAD AND TOBAGO

DUANE 1121/8/

This Instrument was prepared by me,

Attorney-at-Law,

BY THIS POWER OF ATTORNEY given on the *14th* day of *October* In the Year of Our Lord One Thousand Nine Hundred and Eighty-nine, WE **FULTON YORKE** and **GRACE YORKE** of Canaan, Tobago, parents of **DWIGHT YORKE**, a minor do appoint **NEIL WILSON** of Signal Hill, Tobago, to be our Attorney and in our name to do and execute all or any of the following acts,deeds and things that is to say:-

1.	To act on our behalf in all matters pertaining to the welfare of the said **DWIGHT YORKE** until such time as he attains the age of eighteen (18) years.

2.	Specifically to negotiate on our behalf any contract that the said **DWIGHT YORKE** may be offered by **ASTON VILLA FOOTBALL CLUB** of England or by any other Football Club whatsoever and to sign such contract in our name or on our behalf.

3.	To execute and do all other Instruments, acts, deeds and things which our said Attorney shall consider necessary or proper for or in connection with the welfare of the said **DWIGHT YORKE**.

4.	Generally to act in relation to the property affairs or any other matter pertaining to the said **DWIGHT YORKE** as fully and effectually in all respects as we ourselves could do.

.....AND

AND WE hereby undertake to ratify everything which our Attorney or any substitutes or agents appointed by him under the power in that behalf hereinbefore contained shall do or purport to do by virtue of this POWER OF ATTORNEY.

IN WITNESS WHEREOF WE THE SAID FULTON YORKE AND GRACE YORKE have hereunto set our respective hands the day and year first herein-above written.

SIGNED AND DELIVERED by the within-named FULTON YORKE as and for his act and deed in the presence of :

Grace Dennis
Secretary, Scarborough
Tobago

And of me,

Attorney-at-Law

SIGNED AND DELIVERED by the within-named GRACE YORKE as and for her act and deed in the presence of

Grace Dennis
Secretary
Young Street
Scarborough
Tobago

And of me,

Attorney-at-Law.

I, GRACE DENNIS, of Young Street, Scarborough, Tobago, Secretary, make oath and say that I was personally present together with DEBORAH MOORE-MIGGINS, of Young Street, aforesaid on the 14th day of October, 1989, and did then and there see GRACE YORKE and FULTON YORKE parties to the within-written document purporting to be a Power of Attorney and made between the said GRACE YORKE and FULTON YORKE in favour of NEIL WILSON as Attorney sign and deliver the same as and for their respective acts and deeds and that the signatures "Grace Yorke" and "Fulton Yorke" at the foot of the said document subcribed are of the true and proper handwriting of the said "GRACE YORKE" and "FULTON YORKE" and that the signatures "Grace Dennis" and "D.Miggins" also thereto subscribed as those of the witnesses attesting the due execution thereof by the said Grace Yorke and Fulton Yorke in manner aforesaid are of the respective and proper handwriting of me this deponent and of the said DEBORAH MOORE-MIGGINS.

SWORN to at Bacolet Street, Scarborough, Tobago this *14* day of *October* 1989

Before me,

Commissioner of Affidavits

OSCAR DEANE
Commissioner of Affidavits,
Tobago

'She asked if I would be doing the same for my own son, encouraging him in this wild idea. I said I certainly would. If my son decided he wanted to be a janitor, I would do all I could to help him. I then said that if Dwight did make it as a footballer he would earn a great deal more than working in an accounts office.

'Anyway, in the end she did give me permission. "Do what you think best for him," she said. I even got her to sign an affidavit giving me legal powers of attorney to sign things on her behalf.'

Neil went off and returned with a large folder, containing legal and other documents to do with Dwight. The first one, dated 31 January 1989, concerned Dwight's move to Trinidad, when he went to live at Jack Warner's house. Neil had drawn up a very professional-looking letter, ostensibly written and signed by Dwight, but clearly by Neil himself, setting out all the arrangements and agreements for Dwight's training schedules and his schooling in Trinidad.

It stated that Dwight would be allowed to return to Tobago one weekend a fortnight, at the expense of the Trinidad and Tobago Football Association, who would also provide him with out-of-pocket expenses while living in Trinidad. All very efficient. Neil being a businessman, knew that even the most minor matters in any agreement have always to be spelled out clearly, just in case.

Dwight, in this letter supposedly written by him, finishes with quite a flourish. 'I promise to make every effort to co-operate with all concerned in doing such manner of things designed to be mutually beneficial to the Country, the Association and my parents. It is my wish that this move would rebound to the glory and benefit of Trinidad and Tobago.'

Doesn't quite sound like the language of a 17-year-old, but Dwight would doubtless have agreed with the sentiments.

Neil then tried to think of ways of bringing Dwight to the attention of a professional club, using his contacts, such as they were. Very good in Tobago, where he was President of Bertille's coaching clinic, and on the board of various local hotels and businesses, but not so hot outside the island.

'One day, around Chistmas 1988, I heard from someone at the Mount Irvine Bay Hotel that the secretary to the manager of AC Milan was staying there. On holiday. Not business. As a director of the hotel, I made contact with them and got the address and fax number of the AC Milan manager. I sent him a long fax, all about Dwight and his achievements, asking him to give him a trial. They said no. They weren't interested. He wasn't a known name, and they only gave trials to people they'd heard about ...'

Good try, Neil, if rather a long and remote shot. So what luck, some months later, when Aston Villa arrived, in the flesh, able to see and evaluate Dwight at first hand.

I talked to various football experts in Tobago and none could remember a First Division club coming to Tobago before. The nearest was Stoke City, sometime in the 1980s. Since then, none have played in Tobago, or even Trinidad. Whenever British teams visit the West Indies, which is not very often, as Asian or Australian clubs offer better inducements, they normally go to Jamaica or Barbados, better known for their swish hotels than Trinidad or Tobago.

Several Trinidadian players have over the years made it to England and the USA, though none at that stage had made it into the top league or a top team. (Shaka Hislop, now at West Ham, did not arrive at Reading till 1992, via a college in the USA.) In living memory, so I was told, the only Tobagonian to become a professional was John Granville. He played six times for Milwall in 1985.

'When I heard Graham Taylor was interested in Dwight,' says Neil, 'I went to see him at his hotel, Crown Reef. I was also on the board of that hotel.'

Lots of discussions, letters and faxes, then took place, with Neil hoping that Taylor's interest would be formalised and official.

In one letter to Taylor, Neil went over Dwight's career so far, how he'd played for his country since the age of eight, and in various foreign parts.

Graham Taylor had apparently mentioned possible work permit and immigration problems. In this letter Neil Wilson says he had been in touch with Sir Martin Berthoud, the British High Commissioner in Port of Spain, 'who has promised to assist in dealing with any problems that may arise. However, before he could make any move, he will require a firm offer from you inviting Dwight to join your team.'

He also pointed out (hint hint) that Dwight would probably be going to Italy for the World Cup, as one of the stars of Trinidad and Tobago, who seemed likely to reach the finals. The implication being that Villa had a chance to take him, now, while still unknown to the football world.

'It would therefore be useful,' so Neil Wilson ended his letter, 'if you would arrange to let us have this letter so that we could set the wheels in motion to get Dwight to Aston Villa as soon as possible.'

At last, phew, the offer came in writing on 31 July 1989, signed by Graham Taylor. Not to join Villa, but to be given an official trial.

'Dwight will be accompanied by Bertille Sinclair,' so Villa's letter stated. 'Aston Villa will meet half of Mr Sinclair's flight costs and will be responsible for all accommodation expenses of Mr Sinclair and Dwight Yorke during their stay in Birmingham.'

Mr St Clair's name was spelled wrong, but that is a common mistake. In the event, he didn't go. The dates clashed with a summer coaching course Bertille had agreed to attend in the USA. So Neil Wilson went with Dwight. Along with another young player. Villa had decided if they were bringing over one player they might as well have another at the same time, just in case. The other was Colvin Hutchinson. He had played in the Signal Hill Intercol team with Dwight and was also in the Trinidad and Tobago national team.

The flight tickets, arranged by Villa, were economy class. Neil Wilson, being a travel agent, with contacts in many places, got them all upgraded to first class. That's the way to do it. Begin as you mean to go on.

11

When I got offered the trial at Villa, various people tried to talk me out of it. Gully Cummins, the national coach for Trinidad and Tobago, didn't want me to take it. It was such a vital stage for the national team and he didn't want me going away. He wanted me to stay and train with the national team.

Yorke, Hutchinson off to Aston Villa

THE overwhelming support for our footballers, especially from the business community, must be one of the major factors responsible for the restoration of the national team's fortunes as they bid for a place in the World Cup finals next year. And corporate generosity was again in evidence at Crown Point Airport last Sunday evening when a group of well wishers met to bid farewell to Dwight Yorke and Colvin Hutchinson who left the next day for trials with English first division club, Aston Villa.

Yorke's trip was sponsored by the Gulf Insurance Company, and after a desperate appeal by St. Clair Coaching School president Neil Wilson, and an approach to BWIA corporate Manager Peter Ramrattan by Tobago Rotary Club official Ken Sardinha, the national airline agreed to provide tickets for Hutchinson and Wilson to make the trip.

At the local level, a number of business firms, Charmaine's Boutique, Lan Bank, Mt. Irvine Bay Hotel, Sunshine Enterprises and Eddie Pyle all made their contribution to an effort which could culminate with Yorke and Hutchinson becoming the first two home based nationals ever to win contracts with an English first division club.

The youngsters left extremely confident of their chances and that confidence was echoed by Wilson who is convinced that Yorke would return home with a contract and expressed the view that Hutchinson whom he described as "a player of great skill and unflappable temperament" would make a tremendous impression.

The former Signal Hill Senior Comprehensive School midfielders who are both members of the national squad will return at the end of October in time to resume training for the crucial World Cup tie against the USA on November 19.

Colvin Hutchinson (left) and Dwight Yorke (third from left) with Winston Dillon and BWIA Manager Peter Ramrattan (far right).

Other people said much the same, questioning my commitment to my country. The local press had a go at me. It was a hard decision for me. Yeah. A hard time. I was only very young and I felt very emotional about it all. Villa was a big, famous, professional club, where I would have far more opportunities, if of course I made it there. Yet I loved my country. I didn't really want to leave it, except for the sake of my own career.

Anyway, I decided to take the trial, to do what I saw as being best for me.

Neil Wilson, my manager, fixed it all. I don't remember getting any letter offering me the trial. He did all the letters, then told me what the arrangements were. He came with us on the plane. With me and another boy, Colvin Hutchinson.

Colvin was a couple of years older than me. I always thought he was really good. He was from Tobago as well, so that was good for me. He was on the fringes of the national team, not quite a regular. We always thought it a fiddle anyway – calling it the Trinidad and Tobago national team. We'd rarely had many people in it. They always seem to pick people from Trinidad. You had to be really exceptional to get in if you were from Tobago. Colvin hadn't quite established himself, but Graham Taylor had liked the look of him as well.

I bought my first suit in order to go to England. I bought it in Trinidad, in Port of Spain, and it cost TT$800 [about £80]. It was sort of grey. I had a handkerchief sticking out of the top pocket. I thought that would sort of make me look English, help me to fit in. My family bought me a watch as a present. I had no warm clothes at all, as of course we never wore any back home, so I didn't know what to take. I just took my Trinidad national track suit, which I'd got free. I hoped that would keep me warm.

It was brilliant on the plane – it was BA and our tickets were first class. I'd been on planes before, round the Caribbean with the national team, but never to Europe and never first class. I just ate, the whole journey. I just stuffed myself, all the time. It was great.

We were met at Heathrow by Jim Paul, Villa's kit man. He had the club's little minibus and he drove us up to Birmingham.

All I can remember was thinking it's bloody cold. It was all so grey and the clouds were very thick. This must have been in September some time. Can't remember the exact date.

I remember the drive as being very long. Yeah, the plane journey had been longer, but that was exciting, with all the food. I just didn't think the road journey would take that long. In Tobago, there are no long drives. You can drive the whole length of the island in about an hour. So it seemed to take forever and forever, just getting up to Birmingham.

We went to Jim's house in a little village called Shustoke. Just about a 20-minute drive from Villa's training ground. His house was nice, a little cottage. So was the village. I hadn't known what to expect in England, or been told where we would stay, what we would do. But the village turned out to be very beautiful. I suppose you'd call it a sort of typical English village.

We stayed at Jim's house, me and Colvin, for the whole five weeks. Neil Wilson went back after a few days, having seen us settled.

The training ground seemed amazing. I'd never seen a professional set up before. So everything about it was new. And it was all so much bigger and better than I'd expected.

At Bertille's coaching clinic, we never had enough balls for training. And we were always waiting for people to turn up. Players were late, got lost, had no transport or couldn't get off work. This was all so organised, with so many facilities.

And they gave you food as well! That was something I hadn't expected. They had their own restaurant, at the training ground. And the food was free. I stuffed myself every lunchtime.

During the five weeks, we just trained every morning, had lunch, then came back to the digs. I either slept or watched television and ate a lot of chocolate. That's all I did.

I've always had a sweet tooth. And I was coming across so many different bars of chocolate I'd never seen before. I enjoyed watching the TV as well. I remember thinking Only Fools and Horses was really good.

I thought we would stand out at training, among all the English lads, and perhaps be picked upon, but we weren't. There were already lots of black players there, from England of course. But everyone was so busy just getting on with things, that people didn't pay a lot of attention to us in training.

Afterwards, when me and Colvin talked to each other, they couldn't understand our accents. And I couldn't understand a lot of what they said, when they were speaking to each other.

I made friends with Brian Small, who was exactly my age. He was from Birmingham and had played for England Youth. I think he was still a youth trainee at the time. He was very kind and helpful and we're still good friends.

There was no special training for us. We trained with everyone else, did what they did. But they all seemed bigger and stronger and quicker than me. No, I didn't feel out of my depth, not as far as football skills were concerned. I suppose I was also more laid back than them. Too laid back, probably. When I lost the ball, I didn't bother to get it back. That was how we all played in Trinidad and Tobago. The English boys had already been trained to fight to get the ball back.

When it came to actual little matches, I thought I did well. I had a game against Telford and I scored four goals. I could have got ten – but I wasn't really bothered.

Colvin played midfield and I thought he'd done as well as me. So did he. He's very quiet. I suppose I'm a bit cheekier, but we got on well during those five weeks, being together all the time, sharing the same bedroom.

At the end of the five weeks, we both expected to be taken on. I was called in first by Mr Taylor, into his office. He said I was being taken – but not Colvin. He told me before he told Colvin. I suppose he wanted me to understand, and know the reasons.

He said it was because Colvin was two years older, already 20, I think, while I was still 17. He thought I had potential and could be trained, but Colvin was a bit too old for that. At the age of 20, I should be up to scratch. I would have adapted to English ways, the food and the climate. But it was too late for Colvin.

What did I think? I thought that was all crap, just an excuse not to take Colvin.

Bon Accord School teams, Tobago: (Above) Dwight aged eight is in the front row, far right. (Below) Dwight is in the front row, second from the left. KENNETH CROOKS

Dwight receiving the Trinidad and Tobago Secondary Schools Football League trophy on behalf of Signal Hill Senior Comprehensive School in 1989. *TRINIDAD GUARDIAN*

Ten years later, Dwight doing the presenting. Handing the T and T Prime Minister, Basdeo Panday, an autographed copy of Manchester United's victorious team.
TRINIDAD GUARDIAN

Graham Taylor, manager of Aston Villa, who discovered Dwight while on tour in the West Indies, in 1989. COLORSPORT

'Deadly' Doug Ellis, Villa chairman. EMPICS

Ron Atkinson, Villa manager who dropped Dwight. ACTION PLUS

Brian Little, Villa manager who believed in Dwight. COLORSPORT

(Above) John Gregory, Villa manager who sold Dwight to Manchester United in 1998 – and also wanted to 'shoot him'. COLORSPORT

(Left) Andy Comyn, Dwight's room-mate when he moved into more permanent digs in the countryside. ASTON VILLA NEWS AND RECORD OFFICIAL PROGRAMME

(Right) Tony Daley, Villa star; Dwight lived in digs at Tony's mother's house on first arriving in Birmingham. COLORSPORT

(Above) Dwight Yorke
with his Carling
Player of the Month
award. EMPICS

(Left) Ugo Ehiogu,
team-mate at Villa.
COLORSPORT

(Right) Dwight Yorke
celebrates winning
the Coca-Cola Cup
with Aston Villa in
1996. ACTION IMAGES

Dwight Yorke: in action for Villa. 'He was our star, our number one player,' said manager John Gregory. Then after nine years he moved on.
ACTION IMAGES

It was terrible for Colvin, though he didn't show much emotion. I was so disappointed for him. The two of us had set off together in life, expecting we would go on together in life. Now his life had been ruined. He wasn't going anywhere. I was up. He was down.

I was thrilled of course, personally. I thought now I'll be able to look after my mother. I'll be able to give her the setup I'd always dreamed about.

12 Colvin Hutchinson was born in June 1969, so he was two and a half years older than Dwight. He came back to Tobago – to nothing very much. Neil Wilson got him a job at the airport, in a clerical capacity.

'I really thought I'd done enough,' so Colvin says. 'But they thought Dwight, being younger, could be brought up in their ways. Yes, I did find England cold, but I did try to adapt. The food was fine. I didn't find that a problem. Mr Taylor was a nice feller. No, I have no complaints about him.

'Dwight was always very ambitious, despite being so young. I suppose I was a quieter person. More cool, I like to think.

'But I came back very depressed. It took me a long time to recover. All the hard work I'd put in to get there, then I was back where I'd started.'

Neil Wilson, in those three or four days he had spent in Birmingham, seeing Dwight and Colvin settled in, had worried about Colvin.

'I noticed he was standing around with his hands in his pockets. Because of the cold, of course. It was natural, coming from Tobago. But I told him not to – not during training.

'Dwight never did that. He was just as cold, but right from the beginning, he had made up his mind to overcome everything, whatever it was, the cold, the food, the language. Nothing was going to to get him down.

'But at the time, I considered Colvin was just as good as Dwight. In fact there were several others with more natural talent than Dwight. What Dwight had was commitment. When he got his chance, he took it with both hands. And I also like to think he had good guidance ...'

Unbeknown to Dwight, or later forgotten by him, there were several problems which came up during those five weeks of the trial. Some officials at the Trinidad and Tobago FA maintained that Dwight should not be at Aston Villa at all. It wasn't just that they wanted him to remain in Trinidad, to prepare for the World Cup, but that he had gone without authority. They had that authority, not Neil Wilson.

'I denied all this,' says Neil Wilson. 'I had perfect juris-diction to do what I did. But half way through the trial, an official got on to Dwight and said he had to come back. He was very confused and very worried. He was seriously thinking he should return.

'I spoke to him for about one and a half hours on the phone, telling him to stay, convincing him it was best for him. I had already been given a hint by Graham Taylor that Dwight was going to be offered a contract, though I didn't tell Dwight.'

Faxes flew back and forward between Villa and the Trinidad and Tobago FA. In one from Graham Taylor, dated 13 October 1989, he said Villa had broken no rules, had kept all parties informed about the situation and had told the Trinidad Embassy in Britain about the trial. He also stated that both players would return to Trinidad on 19 October, in time for their vital World Cup qualifying match against the USA.

Before then, Neil Wilson had agreed to fly to Birmingham

again, on 17 October, to discuss and finalise the contract which Villa were going to offer to Dwight.

Until now, Neil had done most of the legal letters and official documents himself. This time he thought he should have an actual lawyer present, to handle the contract.

'I had a senior counsel in mind, but at the last minute, he couldn't make it, so I got someone else.'

The someone else was Deborah Moore-Miggins, LLB (Hons) LLM, LEC, Notary Public and Attorney at Law in Scarborough, Tobago. I know all her qualifications as I have her card in front of me. She was a young and most attractive young lawyer, aged just over 30 at the time, who had not long been in practice on her own.

But what I didn't know, till I had lunch with her, was that she is the sister of Dwight Moore, after whom Dwight was named by his mother Grace. Even more coincidental, another brother is Wendell Moore – the player whom Dwight idolised as a young boy. I suppose, though, in a small island like Tobago, these coincidences do happen.

Deborah is one of nine children, like Dwight, and her father was a truck driver. She went to the same primary school as Dwight, but passed the exam for Bishop's High School, going on to the University of the West Indies to read law, followed by a Master's degree in Canada, then work in New York as a legal officer. The Miggins in her double barrelled name comes from her husband who was born in Guyana then went to Sandhurst.

'It was just a minor little job, going to Birmingham to help on Dwight's contract. At that time, I took anything that came along. But I wanted to help him, get him the best deal I could. Wendell had worked so hard, but it had never come off for him. I thought it might help other guys from Tobago in the future.

'I'd never met Dwight before – and I didn't know till you told me now, where his name had come from. He struck me, when I first saw him, as a very shy boy, but very smiley. The minute you spoke to him, he smiled. The minute you asked him a question, he smiled.

'They were all friendly and hospitable at Villa, both the chairman Mr Ellis and Mr Taylor. No, I can't remember the details of their first offer, but I know I was dissatisfied ...'

'Dissatisfied!' says Neil Wilson. 'I had to stop Deborah from walking out. They were only offering Dwight £20 a week. Deborah told them he could get that working in an office in Tobago. She wasn't having that. She was going straight home. I said let's just go out for lunch, then talk about it.

'We were just dealing with Graham Taylor at first, then later Doug Ellis came into the room. I think he took a fancy to Deborah. Anyway, she got it up to £200 a week, which wasn't bad, starting from £20. We also got all the other things we wanted.'

'Although I don't remember now his exact wages,' says Deborah, 'I do remember wanting them to pay for Dwight's continuing education, to agree to send him to some sort of school or college. I also got them to pay for visits from his family and for him to return to Tobago at regular intervals. He was such a young boy and I didn't want the bonds with his family and with his country to be broken.

'Afterwards, it felt like a job well done. Then we all came home together to Tobago. I never saw Dwight after that, not for about eight years, till I met him one day at the airport.'

Dwight returned to Tobago with his contract all lined up at Villa, but foremost in his mind, and everyone else's in Trinidad and Tobago, was the vital match against the USA.

Just two teams would go through from their Caribbean and North America group to the World Cup finals – not one, as Dwight remembered. Costa Rica was leading the group, and looked certain to qualify. The USA and Trinidad and Tobago were neck and neck for second place, miles ahead of Guatemala and El Salvador. Trinidad had scored more goals than the USA and needed only a draw to go through. The whole island of Trinidad, plus little Tobago, had never experienced such excitement and anticipation for a football match.

13 *The big game against the USA, which would get us through to Italy, was on 19 November 1989. I'll always remember that day. We just needed a draw, one point, and we would have been in Italy, in front of a world audience.*

We got beaten 1–0, and that was it. It was a terrible, terrible disappointment. Perhaps we had all got too confident. I know that the whole nation had got really carried away, thinking we were already there, before the match had begun. The game ended in silence. People just walked away, saying nothing.

I did at least have something to look forward to, unlike all the other players. But there were weeks of delays because of a work permit and other things. I'd been offered the contract, but it all depended on getting a work permit.

I had played for the national team about 16 times by then, which was one of the factors. Anyway, it all came through.

I actually signed the contract on 3 November, my 18th birthday. I had to be classed as a full professional by then, at that age, not a trainee or apprentice.

Details of the contract appeared in the Tobago News, which was a bit embarrassing, as it looked as if I was going to make a fortune. I didn't really take in the full details. I would have signed for nothing.

It says in some British football record books that I was signed from St Clair's, or sometimes it says Signal Hill for £120,000. St Clair's is right, or Signal Hill, as that was where Bertille's coaching club was – but the money's all wrong. I don't know where that figure came from.

YORKE SIGNS $¾m VILLA CONTRACT

By COMPTON DELPH

TOBAGONIANS in all walks of life were jubilant earlier this week when it was announced that their football idol, 17-year-old Dwight Yorke, had signed an agreement for a contract worth more than $800,000 with English First Division club, Aston Villa.

In the making for several weeks now, the final terms of the contract were hammered out last week in England between officials of Aston Villa and Yorke's Manager Neil Wilson, with Attorney-at-Law Mrs. Deborah Moore-Miggins, acting as legal adviser.

And according to Villa's Manager, Graham Taylor, never before had he offered a 17-year-old such a generous contract.

Yorke will get a $40,000 signing on fee, a starting weekly wage of $1,350 increasing to $4,000, bonuses ranging from $1,350 to $17,000 per game, plus such perks as a car, free medical and dental care, insurance coverage, and all expenses "in his pursuit of an education."

Benefitting, too, from the contract will be the local football club, St. Clair Coaching School, which will receive $67,000 for releasing the teenaged star to Aston Villa.

Following is the text of a statement issued earlier this week by Neil Wilson, who is also President of the Coaching School:

"Agreement between Dwight Yorke and Aston Villa Football Club was signed by the parents of Dwight Yorke on behalf of Dwight Yorke and Douglas Ellis, Chairman of Aston Villa on behalf of Aston Villa Football Club of Birmingham, England, giving effect to negotiations conducted in Birmingham on October 18, 1989, between officials of Aston Villa and Yorke's representatives. This agreement forms the basis of a final contract which is being finalised.

"The main features of the contract are as follows:

1. The Contract will take effect from the date when a work permit has been secured and will run until June 30, 1992.
2. Yorke will be paid a signing-on fee of $40,000.
3. All expenses incurred by Yorke in his pursuit of an education will be the responsibility of Aston Villa.
4. Yorke will be paid a basic weekly wage commencing from the date of the work permit starting at $1,350 rising to $4,000, depending on the number of games played.
5. Yorke will be entitled to receive bonuses ranging from $1,350 to $17,000 per game depending on the placing of Aston Villa on the League — FA — Littlewoods Standings.
6. Appearance fees will also be paid to Yorke ranging from $1,350 to $17,000 per game, depending on the placing of Aston Villa on the standings.
7. Yorke will receive $650 for every senior international game in which he participates, and $325 for every Under-21 game in which he plays for his country.
8. He will be adequately covered by insurance at the expense of Aston Villa and during the life of the contract, he will receive free medical and dental care.
9. An injury benefit clause provides for Yorke to be paid all his basic wages for a period of 26 weeks, and for the four games after the game in which he was injured, he will be entitled to all bonuses enjoyed by those players who took part in the four games.
10. Yorke will be provided with four return air tickets from Tobago to Birminham per year for himself and any others nominated by him.
11. A weekly accomodation allowance will be paid to Yorke by Aston Villa.
12. Yorke will be released to play for his country for international games generally. He will be released to join the World Cup squad and the Under-18 camp as specifically requested by Yorke with the approval of the T&TFA.
13. In certain cup matches, Yorke will be entitled to a share of the net receipts of games in which he participates.
14. All gear will be provided by Aston Villa at their expense.
15. All proceeds from endorsements of footwear, clothing, etc., earned by Aston Villa will be shared by Yorke while he is a regular player and nominated to share in this benefit.
16. The contract is subject to review no later than 30th June 1991.

As part of the overall package, a transfer fee of $67,000 will be paid to the St. Clair Coaching School for the release of Yorke.

It was also agreed that as a regular member of the First Team, Aston Villa will make an automobile available to Yorke without cost to Yorke.

During the negotiations, manager Graham Taylor expressed satisfaction with what he had seen of Yorke. He stressed that never before had he offered a 17-year-old such a generous contract and he was the man who signed John Barnes as a 17-year-old to play for Watford.

The total, as I remember it, was only £10,000. Bertille's club got £5,000 up front. I got £2,000 as my share of the transfer fee. The club was to get the remaining £3,000, when I had played a certain amount of games. I also got a £2,000 signing-on fee. My wages were going to be £200 a week, which would go up depending on how many first team appearaces I made. Appearance money was extra, if I got in the first-team. I think it was £250 a game. Then there were win bonuses as well. I don't really remember the details. My contract was for two years. I do remember that. So whatever happened, I would have a decent chance to show what I could do. I couldn't wait ...

Note: The contract made headline news in the *Tobago News* on 27 October 1989, revealing some of the clauses you don't normally read in English papers. Neil Wilson let me see the whole contract, but it was on fax paper and had faded.

The paper said it was worth TT$800,000, which was then equal to around £120,000. (That's possibly where the later mistake stating that the transfer fee was £120,000 came from.) It listed some of Dwight's perks and extras, such as free health and dental care, free football gear, use of a car and accommodation, which no doubt made many readers pretty jealous.

Graham Taylor was quoted as saying it was the most generous contract he had given to a 17-year-old. The paper added that he was the manager who had signed 17-year-old John Barnes for Watford.

Part 2
BIRMINGHAM

Part 2
BIRMINGHAM

14 Aston Villa is one of England's oldest and most famous clubs, a founder member of the world's first Football League in 1888, along with eleven other teams – Accrington Stanley, Blackburn Rovers, Bolton Wanderers, Burnley, Derby County, Everton, Notts County, Preston North End, Stoke, West Bromwich Albion and Wolverhampton Wanderers. Note how they were all from the North and the Midlands. London hardly existed as far as football was concerned.

They were formed in 1874 by a group of cricketing enthusiasts who belonged to the Villa Cross Wesleyan Chapel in Aston, Birmingham. Dwight's mother would have been pleased, if she had been aware of this connection. They wanted to start a football team to give them something to do in the winter, but there were so few other football teams to play against that their first game was against a local rugby club. They played one half rugby, the other half football. A novel idea, which didn't quite catch on. Then a Scotsman called George McGregor Ramsay arrived, knocked them into shape as a proper football club, and in ten years they were established enough to join the new national league.

In the 1890s, they were the nation's foremost club, winning the League championship five times and the FA

Cup three times. For almost the next 100 years, their progress was not quite so spectacular. They had spells in the Second Division in the 1930s and in the 1950s, dropped to the Third Division in 1971, but then stormed back in 1981 and surprised the football world by winning the First Division title. The next year they did even better – winning the European Cup.

That was their peak, so far, from where they fell yet again, dropping into Division Two in 1987. But they were there for only one season as Graham Taylor got them promoted in 1988. When Dwight arrived at the end of 1989, they were looking to confirm this position as a strong First Division Club. (Or Premier League, as it became in 1992.)

Villa have always liked to consider themselves the main Midlands club, with a classier following and a more distinguished history than their Birmingham rivals, though West Brom, fellow founders of the Football League, have also won the League once, back in 1920. Birmingham City, an equally ancient club, have never won it. Their best was sixth in 1956. Like Wolves, another historic club, City have been stuck in the lower divisions in recent decades.

Villa's strip is known throughout the football world, being a rather tasteful combination of claret and blue. Until the present-day rise to world domination of Manchester United, Villa's strip was one of the most popular British strips. Foreigners bought it not because of Villa's fame but because it looked nice.

But perhaps the best-known feature of Aston Villa, in the minds of neutral supporters, is Doug Ellis, or Deadly Doug, as he is known, a footballing legend, in the Midlands at least, ever since Jimmy Greaves gave him his nickname.

Doug Ellis, now in his 70s, made his fortune in the travel trade in Birmingham. Before the war, he played football himself, as an amateur for Southport, though he only managed a couple of games. During the war, he served in the Navy. 'I don't want to name drop, but one of the people

I served with in the same waters was the Duke of Edinburgh.'

When he left the Navy, with a gratuity of £300, he decided to go into the travel business. 'A lot of the people I'd served with used to say they'd like to come back to Europe and the Far East, once the war was over, even the ones who could probably never even have filled in their passport forms.'

He started with a travel firm in Preston, moving to Birmingham in 1948, eventually setting up on his own. 'I remembered the charabanc trips which travel agents organised before the war, to places like Morecambe and Blackpool. I thought I'd try to do the same with Europe. I hired a Dakota and organised a trip to France, doing everything myself, with my wife, from the food to the hotel. That first trip sold so well that in a year or so I was running 27 flights a week. In 1962 I sold out for a lot of money. I then went into property, houses, hotels and farms. I sold most of that in 1976.'

So, he was already a pretty wealthy businessman when he became chairman of Aston Villa in 1968. He's been chairman ever since – except for a short spell of three years between 1979 and 1982, during which time Villa won the League and the European Cup. What went wrong, Doug? 'I had a difference of opinion with my fellow directors, that was all.' Today, back in control, he owns 38.6 per cent of the shares.

He doesn't seem to mind being known as Deadly. He used it as the title of an autobiography which was published by a Birmingham firm in 1998. 'No use you trying to buy a copy. It's sold out. I'm a bestseller, just like my friend Jeffrey Archer ...'

The 'Deadly' comes from his habit of sacking managers. 'I've only sacked seven in 30 years,' he told me. 'That's not bad.'

Yes, but how many managers have you had at Villa in that time? 'Eleven. John Gregory is my 12th. He's a good manager, so I hope I won't have to sack him. I hate sacking managers, I really do.'

Not all of course were sacked, not even in the technical sense. That's just Doug getting carried away with being Deadly Doug. But quite a few were, enough for him to deserve his soubriquet.

Doug was on that little tour of Trinidad and Tobago and remembers clearly, so he says, what happened.

'It was on a summer tour, before the season began. I don't remember the first match in Trinidad, at least I don't remember Dwight being outstanding, but I do remember the Tobago game. It was in a sort of playing field, a park pitch, without a stadium, and we were sitting on benches beside the pitch.

'I was sat next to Graham and after about 10 minutes I said, "Heh, look at that feller, the one with a number 8 on his back" – I think it was 8 – "by God he can play." I walked to the other bench, where the Tobago coach was, and I said, "How old is your number 8?" They said 16. I said, "Any honours?" They said, "yes." I said, "Has he played for the Under 18s?" They said, "yes – and the Under 21s and the full national side." "My God," I said, "and he's only 16." As it happens, it turned out later he was 17. But it was still amazing. He did look so very young.

'I remember sending the plane tickets for them to come over. I have a memory of his aunt coming with him. I think I've got that right. She was a barrister, and she fell in love with me, so I was told.

'There was another boy. I can't remember his name but Graham didn't think he was good enough.

'The official signing-on fee for Dwight was only £10 – but I gave his local club £10,000. They were only a little club and needed the money.

'Straight away, Dwight became my son. Oh yes. That's

how I looked upon him. We're a family club here. I always looked upon him as one of my own sons.

'He wasn't very well organised when he came here, and very thin. In fact, he was a very skinny lad. It's their upbringing, you see. We in the Western world have all the vitamins we want, but out there, perhaps they don't. He was from a big family, with five or six brothers I think it was. They were very poor and had to catch crabs. So you can understand why he was so skinny. But you have to hand it to him. He worked hard in the gym, built himself up, made his upper body very strong, which is what you need for a footballer.'

Did you think he would do as well as he has done?

'In 30 years in football, I've seen lots of lads who are good at 16 or 17, then they drop. Sometimes they come back at 20, 21, but often they don't. They disappear.

'With Dwight, I thought he's got a chance, and I'll tell you why. He was hungry. Dwight was hungry. We suffer today because too many kids have it too easy. They don't try hard enough, eat the wrong diet. Dwight also had confidence. So there you have it – Dwight had hunger and confidence. And the will to succeed.

'He grew to be one of the best and most popular players. He certainly became more popular than Ron Atkinson, but we won't go into that ...'

Graham Taylor's memory of discovering Dwight is not totally the same as Mr Ellis's. Deborah was of course not Dwight's aunt, and he laughed at the idea of Deborah falling for Doug Ellis. 'I suspect it was the other way round. But she was very attractive and intelligent. I only wish I could meet some more lawyers and agents like her today ...'

He also smiled at Doug's suggestion that it was he, Doug Ellis, who first noticed Dwight. 'He said that? Well who am I to argue with Doug Ellis, but don't you think it would be more likely that it was me, as manager, who said to Doug, "that lad looks good," rather than the other way round?'

Most interesting of all was Graham's correction about the date of Villa's tour of Trinidad. Doug Ellis had remembered it as a pre-season, summer tour. Dwight himself had thought it was in the summer, some time.

'No it wasn't,' says Graham.

'It was early March 1989. We played Spurs on the Wednesday, then because all Saturday matches had been put off, because of an England game, we had about ten days free. This was in the early days of Premier games being postponed to help England.

'We had just come up into the First Division and were still struggling to find our feet. When I saw the gap coming up, I decided we should have a short, mid-season break.

'I don't know how we came to go to Trinidad and Tobago. I just wanted us to get away somewhere. We only played the two matches. It was booked up at the last minute, probably just two or three weeks before. I should think it was the only place we could find, at short notice ...'

So that explains the sudden and unusual appearance of a top English club. And points out how lucky Dwight was – to have been there, in the right place at the right time.

'I do remember the discussions about Dwight playing for us in the second half. I spoke to their officials about it at half time. They felt that if Dwight scored for us, which was likely, and therefore helped to beat Tobago, the crowd would be very unhappy. It would be hard for Dwight to live with afterwards. People wouldn't forget it. So when this was pointed out, I agreed that he should stay on their side.

'But I had not the slightest doubts about his talent. You don't have to be an expert to recognise such natural ability. In the second half, I hoped he wouldn't play as well.'

Why ever not?

'I didn't know who else was in the ground, did I? It was just a little park, but you never know. "I wonder who's here."

That was what I thought. I didn't want anyone else to see him.'

So why did it take so long – from first spotting him in March to giving him a trial in September?

'Oh work permits and things, then the summer came. I wanted to hurry it because I was told he might be going to the USA on a sports scholarship. I don't know whether that was true, or was just to make us hurry up.'

Why was Colvin asked as well?

'Oh he looked useful. But I also thought having two together would help them over here, and help us. I hadn't ruled Colvin out, when he came for the trial, oh no. But Dwight was the special one. No question about that.

'The changing room at our training ground was about 200 yards from the pitch and I remember Dwight walking those 200 yards with the ball balanced on his head, all the way. Incredible.

'Now does that show you are going to be a footballer? Does it heck. Of course it doesn't. But it does show you have a gift with a ball, and that you love it.

'I saw that in Tobago. He could shield the ball, lay it off, but most of all, what he had was timing. Now you can teach lots of things, but you can't teach that sort of timing.

'When I first saw him in Tobago, there was a tingle up my spine. You don't often feel that in football ...'

I arrived in Birmingham in December 1989. I was on my own this time. It was just before Christmas. The club fixed me up with digs in the middle of Birmingham with Tony Daley's mother.

Tony Daley was an established player in the first team. He was about four years older than me, I think. No, he wasn't there. He didn't live at home any more. He had his own place somewhere else. It was a mainly black area of Birmingham. I didn't like it there. It was quite tough. I didn't feel safe. You had to look over your shoulder all the time.

But my biggest problem was the climate. It was just so cold. I was freezing all the time.

I only stayed at Mrs Daley's about six weeks. Then I moved to some other digs, with Sheila and Bryn, back in Shustoke, the same little village I'd stayed in with Jim Paul during my trial. Sheila's house was very nice. A typical English cottage.

I was glad to be out of the city, out of Birmingham. And I loved it with Sheila and Bryn, right from the beginning.

There was another Villa player staying with them when I arrived, Andy Comyn. We shared a bedroom. He had lots of 'O' levels and 'A' levels and I don't know what else. A very clever man. He helped me a lot, explained things I didn't understand about England.

We didn't have a car for a few weeks, so it was hard getting to the training ground. Then Villa gave us an old car, a red Montego, which me and Andy shared. We took it in turns to have it. Yes, I could drive. I'd passed my test in Tobago, but I'd never had a car of my own.

I'd only been at Sheila's a few weeks when I woke up one day and saw all this snow outside. I'd never seen snow, of course. It was a real blizzard. I thought I'll go back to bed and keep warm, no one will be training in this.

About an hour later, Dave Richardson, the youth team development officer, was on the phone, asking where the hell I was. I couldn't believe English people trained in such weather. Training in the cold and rain had been bad enough – but I didn't think we'd actually be training when there was thick snow on the ground.

It was hard driving through the snow to get to the training ground. I was really scared. I didn't know how you drove in snow. So I just went really, really slowly ...

I don't remember finding the training difficult, or getting worried about it. I've always been fairly confident. It all just seemed so exciting.

I loved it all, everything about it, once I settled at Sheila and Bryn's ...

16 When Dwight said he moved into 'a typical English cottage', I didn't quite believe it. What did he know about English cottages, coming from the Caribbean? It must be a phrase he'd picked up. Probably a boring little semi, or a council house on an estate.

It turned out to be a yummy, picture-book cottage, deep in rural Warwickshire, sixteenth century, lots of beams and period features, with a pretty, old-fashioned garden, two orchards, surrounded by fields filled with horses and cattle.

The village of Shustoke is small, just a few dozen houses and one pub, the Plough. No signs of any nasty motorways or modern developments, yet taking the rural back doubles, Villa's training ground at Bodymoor Heath is only 20 minutes away.

Sheila and Bryn Dudley are in their early 60s, each well-built, homely country folks, born and brought up locally. They have been married for 30 years and have no children.

'Except Dwight,' said Sheila.

She was having her hair done when I arrived, sitting in the kitchen where a girl was putting in her curlers.

Bryn, now retired through ill health, was a long-distance coach driver. Sheila used to work part time at Villa's training ground in their restaurant.

'When Graham Taylor arrived, he closed down the hostel where young players having trials used to stay. So they had to find local digs for them. Bryn was away a lot at the time, on the continent, so I said yes, I'd take some, though I didn't know what on earth I was supposed to do with them. That first time, I took six.'

Not all at the same time, surely, in such a small cottage?

'Oh we have three bedrooms. I put four single beds in one bedroom, and two in another. Oh bags of room.'

The charge to the club was £10 a night, for bed and breakfast, an evening meal and doing their washing. Today it's £12 a night.

'The biggest problem with young boys is always the same – their food. The club wants them to eat sensible, lots of vegetables and pasta. All they like is junk food. That's the way they've been brought up. I blame their parents. I tell them they won't have energy to make it as a footballer, if they don't eat their greens. They all moan, but I don't stand any nonsense.

'The worst that's happened, so far, is four lads who helped themselves to Bryn's drinks. He has his own cocktail bar in a corner of the lounge with about 100 bottles of all sorts, mostly brought back from abroad.

'We had four boys at the time, all from Scotland. I told the club – and all four were expelled. They never got another club.'

How about girls?

'Oh we don't allow them, not in their rooms.'

One day, in January 1990, Sheila got a call from someone at the club. 'He said it was very urgent. They had to find a home for this boy in 24 hours – or he's going home.

' "There's another thing I must tell you," he said. "He's from the Caribbean." I said I'd have to ask my husband. Bryn was on the continent at the time, in Austria, but I knew his hotel.'

'When I heard,' says Bryn, 'I said I don't care about where he's from. Makes no difference to me. As long as he's clean, tidy and respects my home. Otherwise, he'll feel my ten size boot up his jaxie.'

'Dwight arrived the next morning at 7.30. No, hold on, I think it was nearer 7.45, but I can remember it to this day. Oh what a sad little boy he looked. So thin and miserable. He had about ten bags of his dirty washing. I said give them to me, love. Don't you worry. Just go off to training, and when you come back, love, I'll have a nice meal for you.

'When he came back that day, I had most of his washing done. He gave me a smile when he came through that door – and he didn't stop smiling in all the years he stayed here. Or since.

'Oh he was so young, so innocent. I said to him if he ever had any, you know, man's problems, he could talk to Bryn ...'

And did he have any manly problems for Bryn to deal with?

'No, but eventually we did hear about his problems at Mrs Daley's. Personally, and this is just my opinion, I think some people were a bit jealous of Dwight, that he would take Tony's place in the team. I don't think enough was done for him. He was on his own over Christmas. Terrible. No wonder he was so unhappy and wanted to go home.'

'In the early weeks, we found it difficult at times to understand his accent. He couldn't understand some things we said either. He once came back from training and asked me what it meant "to get a bollocking". Another time he was worried about the word greedy. He'd been told to be "greedy on the ball" and had not heard that phrase before.

'For the first two weeks or so, when he didn't have a car, I drove him to training. As I let him out he'd give me a kiss. When it first happened, I thought, "Oh my God, if the other players see that, they'll tease him rotten." But he didn't care. He kisses people all the time and cuddles them. I expect in a big family he didn't get a lot of time and attention.'

'He did try to kiss me,' says Bryn, 'but I told him to piss off.'

'If any local kids came round,' says Sheila, 'he'd play with them outside on the lawn. At any sport, he always wanted to do well – football, table tennis, darts or whatever.'

'He's always been very kind and generous, even when he had little money, he was sending some to his mother.

' "Mums," he said to me once, as we were walking through the village. "Do you fancy an ice-cream?" So we went to the shop and he bought three ice-creams. I said why three. He'd seen a man working in his garden on the way to the shop, so on the way back, he gave the man an ice-cream.

'He's always cheerful and very loving. Personally, I think it's because he had a hard life at home in Tobago. He rarely talks about his home life. And I don't think I ever heard him mention his father.

'He only had one pair of shoes to his name when he arrived – and I think they were hand-me-downs. He did come from a very poor family. His feet are still twisted, if you look at them. I blame all those years wearing someone else's shoes.'

'What I've always liked about him,' says Bryn, 'is that he can take a joke. I remember he was once sitting near that window, with his back to it. It was a really bright sunny morning and I said to Dwight, what's the matter, are you worried about being sunburned? He laughed at that.'

'The first girl he was interested in was Emma, the girl next door,' says Sheila.

'He asked if I could get a rose for her. When I got him a rose, he said to me, "Mums, could you go and put it on Emma's doorstep?" Oh he always called me Mums. Still does.

'He always had a ball with him. He kept one in his bedroom, all the time. I remember when he first came hearing this sort of funny noise in his bedroom and wondering what it was. What he was doing was lying in bed, on his back, throwing the ball in the air. Then he'd catch it on his neck, or head. Hour after hour. He literally did sleep with a ball. When I made his bed, I'd leave his ball on his pillow.

'Another funny thing, when he first came, was when we heard him talking to someone in his room – yet there was no one there. It turned out to be his prayers. He always said them, last thing at night. No, he didn't go to church. I don't think we've got his sort of church, not round here.

'He was always a slow eater. If Dwight had a spud left on his plate, Andy would pick it up and eat it. Dwight would just laugh.'

Andy Comyn was aged 21 when Dwight arrived at Sheila's. So he was three years older. And from a different background. Not just from Dwight, but from your normal, average footballer, not many of whom have degrees. He was born in Wakefield in 1968, his father, also a graduate, was in the wine business. Aged 15, he signed as a school boy with Manchester United.

'All the time I was at Manchester United, I made it clear that if my "A" levels were good enough, I wanted to go to university. They didn't actually offer me professional forms, but I did get good "A" levels. I went to Birmingham University to read physics. While there, I continued to play for Manchester United, for the A and B teams, as a non-professional.

'Then I got a serious back injury and was out for four months. By that time, Ron Atkinson had been sacked. When Alex Ferguson arrived, he released me. He didn't know who I was. I was still injured and hadn't played for them for a long time. I had no complaints.'

After he recovered from his injury, he played for Birmingham University and then represented British Universities. In his spare time, he played non-league football for Alvechurch.

'But I still had a yearning to play pro football, before I went into some sort of career. I wrote to Wolves and Villa, asking for a trial. I shouldn't have done, as I had signed for Alvechurch, but I wasn't aware of the rules.

'Anyway, Wolves never replied – but Villa did. I was offered a week's trial – which coincided with the first day of my finals, so I couldn't make that trial.'

He took his exams – graduating with a 2:2, not bad for a footballer – and Villa put back his trial. They looked at him for three weeks – and offered him a two-year contract.

'I signed on 18 August 1989, aged 21. The club fixed me up with digs at Sheila's. On 21 August, I played for Villa's reserves. Then on the twenty-third, I made my first-team debut against Liverpool. I'd gone from non-league to playing against Liverpool in one week.'

So that's how Dwight came to be sharing with an older player from a middle-class background. A late starter, but one who had suddenly caught up, just as Dwight arrived.

But although Andy had got into the first-team squad, he was not quite a regular. Paul McGrath was the first choice for his position in central midfield.

What did Andy think of young Yorke when he suddenly arrived in his digs?

'Actually, I remember him earlier, during his five-week trial with the other boy. Can't remember his name now. I hadn't been on the trip to Trinidad, so I hadn't seen him play before, which the other players had. Yeah, I was most impressed by Dwight's ball skills. He could run with the ball on his head, which was amazing.

'We got on very well at Sheila's. We became the two permanent guests. In the afternoons, after training, we'd go into Birmingham together, look at the clothes shops. We didn't get recognised of course. Nobody knew us. Dwight was very keen on tracksuits, the flashier the better. He bought about four. When he went back to Tobago to see his family, he came back with none. He'd given them to all his friends.

'We'd go to McDonald's together and Dwight would have a thick shake. Yeah, I would as well. During those 18 months or so living with Dwight, I probably put on five or six pounds. Normally I never never put on weight, though I do eat a lot.

'No, I wasn't pinching stuff from Dwight's plate. It was because he was a slow eater – and hadn't got used to English food. At breakfast, we often got toast and Marmite. Dwight had never heard of it – so I'd eat it up for him.

'Everyone at the club knew him for his smile, and his white teeth. I think he partly played up the smiley bit – but that's his nature. Except when he was down. Oh yes. He did have lows.

'Back in Tobago, he had been a star, known by everyone. At Villa he was unknown, and very junior. Dwight couldn't take it when he wasn't picked for a team, or got dropped. No player can take that. Even senior players don't always get such things explained to them. It should always be explained. This is one of the faults of British football. But with someone like Dwight, he got confused and upset. "What have I got to do to be picked? What do I do to make myself better? How can I improve? How can I show them – if I'm not in the team."

'Those were the sort of things he'd say to me back at Sheila's, then flop in front of the TV.'

Did he strike you as intelligent, sharp, clever or what?

'As a footballer he was bright and sharp, with a good football brain. As a person, he wasn't thick, but don't forget he was a foreigner who had just arrived. He'd ask me lots of questions about British things, British traditions and phrases.'

Dwight was lucky then, having an educated room mate, who was prepared to explain things to him. At the club itself, Andy was naturally mocked and teased for being an educated posho.

'My nickname at the club was Jeeves. Dennis Booth, the Villa coach, first called me that. It became my dressing-room name. I'm still known by that, when I meet any old Villa players.

'I suppose what I remember most about him, from those

early months, was basically how confident he was. We used to have what we called the long run, which was six laps round the track. Gordon Cowans held the record. Dwight was very confident he could beat it. He started off at a great pace. After two laps, he was miles behind. It wasn't arrogance, his boasting. Looking back, he was just naïve, over enthusiastic.'

Dwight was a bit hurt by this story when I told him. 'Yeah, I can remember that incident, but I didn't realise it was so windy that day. Half way round I ran into a brick wall. That was the real reason.

'When I used to say those sort of things, I was really just testing myself.

'As for the ball tricks, running or walking with the ball on my head. I never practised them. Honestly. I just felt confident I could do them.'

Tony Daley, one of the stars in Villa's first team when Dwight arrived, has similar memories of Dwight's confidence, and his party tricks.

He was four years older than Dwight, born in Birmingham of West Indian parents. His mother and father had both come from Jamaica in the 1950s. A bit like Dwight in build, being medium height and fairly slight, and also with a high degree of skill. He played on the wing and had represented England at Youth and B international level, going on in due course to play for the full England team.

'Dwight struck most players, how shall I say this, not as arrogant, but very confident of his own ability. He would talk about his career, how he would do this and that, be in the first team by a certain time, have a car and house, all that stuff. It wasn't really boasting, just natural confidence.

'We would take the piss of course, as all players do, trying to cut him down to size. But it was amazing, all that confidence, when you think of the little place he'd come from, and he'd only been here ten minutes. But everyone liked him, no question. He was a smashing lad.

'I can remember him on a sunny day playing in his full track suit and gloves – yet we were all sweltering. I wouldn't say he was frail, but it was clear he'd have to be stronger to survive.

'What amazed us all was his ball juggling. One day he bet one of the senior players – can't remember who – that he could stand in a dustbin and do 100 headers. He got to number 96 without a mistake, then he slowly let the ball roll from his head down the front of his face. As it passed his lips, he kissed the ball. He rolled it back up – and finished his 100 headers. Everyone laughed and cheered. Probably a few jeered as well. As footballers do.

'People took the mickey out of his West Indian accent, but you have to live with that. All footballers pick on something. As I've moved around, people have always had a go at my Birmingham accent. You just have to accept it.

'I became quite friendly with him, so it was probably that which made Graham Taylor think he might feel at home with my mother. I suppose he thought a West Indian family would make Dwight feel at home. My mother hadn't taken in young footballers before. It was the club's idea, and she said yes. I wasn't living at home, so I don't know what happened.'

Dwight couldn't remember the address, or had wiped it from his mind, but Tony says it was a two-storey council house in a fairly tough area of Birmingham.

'I think he was happy enough initially, but well, I think he could have been happier elsewhere ...'

I said that Dwight remembers being a bit frightened, that he found walking around at night sometimes pretty scary.

'When I lived there, growing up, I didn't think that. It just seemed sort of normal. But it's true when I go back there today, yeah, even I find it a bit tough. Let's say you have to know how to look after yourself.

'Coming from the quiet place he came from, I can understand that. I do admire what he did, how he survived.'

Did it ever strike you that Dwight might be a rival, and eventually take your place in the team?

'Not at all. I was much older than him, well established. The thought never struck me. I played on the wing. He did, from time to time, but he didn't like that and much preferred playing up front in the middle.

'I admired his skill. We were in a friendly once, against some local Midlands team. I can't remember who it was now, but we were meant to take it seriously. We were about eight or nine goals up and Dwight went racing down the field, beat several players, beat the goalie, then beat him again, just show-boating. Then when he had an empty goal he put it wide. He was dragged straight off for that ...'

My first appearance in the first team was in March 1990. I'd been playing for the reserves, but travelling with the first team as a squad player for the two months or so since I'd arrived.

Mr Taylor made me a sub for the match against Crystal Palace, at Selhurst Park. He didn't tell me I'd be on the bench, not until about an hour before. He said he was making me sub because the West Indies were beating England that day at cricket and I might bring the team good luck.

I was excited, but I don't remember being nervous, or all jitters. I've always been a cool customer, laid back. I don't know whether *it's to protect myself or not. It's just me. It's not being over confident or cocky. Just, well, cool.*

I only came on for 15 minutes. We got beaten. I think it was 1–0 to them.

I made just one other first-team appearance as sub that season. At the time, you only had two subs sitting on the bench, plus the goalies, not five like today.

I made my full debut the following season, 1990–91, and that was against Manchester United. So I'm told. I can't actually remember that game, but I didn't do very well. That was when Tommy Docherty made that remark about me.

Funnily enough I can remember more about a match against Manchester City. Peter Reid was playing for them that day.

In that first season, I was just a kid of 18, whom nobody knew, and I had cost the club nothing really.

But I thought I'd done quite well that first season, coming on twice as sub. Not as often as I'd hoped, but not bad.

Then Graham Taylor left Villa. That was terrible for me. He left to take on the England job, so good for him. But not for me. I'd only been there six months. Now he was gone, the person who had found me and encouraged me, who'd been responsible for me coming to England.

Most people in football still didn't know who I was. And they had no idea where Tobago was. The ones who had heard of Tobago, thought of cricket, not football. When I told new people, when I met them for the first time, they didn't believe we played football there.

So yeah, I was very worried. I thought that's it, I wouldn't make any more progress. Especially when I heard the next manager was going to be Dr Venglos. I hadn't heard of him, so I was pretty sure he would not have heard of me ...

18

Although Dwight can't remember much about those first six months, except the dramatic news that his manager, creator and father figure had moved off and away, Rob Bishop has all the details safe in his little note book.

'Dwight played for just eight minutes on his debut at Crystal Palace on 29 March 1990. He came on in the 82nd minute as a substitute for Tony Daley.'

Hmm, interesting, Rob, glad you had that tucked away.

'The following week, in a 2–1 home defeat by Manchester City, on 1 April 1990, he replaced Ian Ormondroyd, all 6ft 5in of him, in the 76th minute.

Thanks, Rob.

Mr Bishop, 49, is the Chief Football Reporter for the *Birmingham Post*. Before that he was on the *Birmingham Evening Mail* and before that the *Wolverhampton Express and Star*. But the *Dudley Herald* was where he began, as a tea boy. So, he has been covering football in the Birmingham area for over 30 years.

Since 1987, he has kept his own handwritten book of records – on all games played by the four main Midlands clubs: the scores, who played, who got

Villa put Trinidad teenagers on trial

14 SEP 1989

By ROB BISHOP

● Aston Villa are giving month-long trials to two players who could be playing in next summer's World Cup Finals.

● Teenager striker Dwight Yorke and midfielder Colvin Hutchinson are members of the Trinidad and Tobago side who will qualify for Italy if they win their remaining group match against USA.

School

● "They came to our attention when we played a Tobago XI on our trip to the West Indies in March," said Villa manager Graham Taylor.

● "Yorke really took the eye, although he was still at school then, so we invited them over.

● "They will be spending four weeks with us, although they will not be able to play in competitive matches because they do not have work permits."

booked. Surely a bit unnecessary, when such records are in all the papers?

'Ah but I find it more reliable to keep my own. You'll also find that papers don't keep the total of bookings. They can be very useful ...'

In 1989, he remembers going to Villa's training ground and catching his first sight of the recently arrived Dwight.

'He was so slight and slender, a little boy lost. On the training ground, his skill was incredible, but I doubted if he would be strong enough for the very physical nature of English football.

'In his early years, he was always doing lots of tricks. I remember him once having a bet with a senior player, Bosnich I think it was, that he could head the ball 100 times – standing in a doorway. In the open air, you have more chance, because you can head the ball up to the sky. In a doorway, you have only a couple of feet in which to manoeuvre. He did it, of course, no problem.'

Rob wrote a piece in the *Evening Mail* on 16 September 1989 about Dwight and Colvin being given a trial – and spelled both their names correctly. Not always the case. Even when Dwight had got into the first team, Yorke still often came out as York.

That was the first mention of Dwight in an English paper. Dwight hasn't of course got that cutting. He's never kept any. When he arrived, he arrived with nothing, no papers, no photos, no personal memorabilia, and has picked up no such stuff on his travels since. Very thoughtless. How did he expect a biographer to cope? Surely when he was imagining himself making it, he was also seeing the hacks, hanging on his every word?

'I know why he remembers that Manchester City match,' says Graham Taylor.

'He was supposed to be picking up Peter Reid. That was the job I gave him. But he didn't. When I see him now, I remind him of it. But no, I didn't give a rollicking. In the six months or so I had him, I only had occasion to do it once, only once that I spoke to him sternly. Nothing serious. Just to put more into his game.

'He wasn't a lad who needed a rollicking. More an arm round his shoulder. He could let little things get to him, but he had done so well, surviving the culture shock of coming to England. No, he didn't need rollickings.

'My biggest regret in leaving Villa was Dwight. No, honestly. I said to Rita, my wife, that's what I really regret. I'm leaving behind someone who is going to be a world-class player.'

The next manager, Dr Venglos, who arrived in time for the new season, 1990–91, soon had more things to worry about than potential. His worry was the here and now, getting results, before the team started sliding down the League.

But Dwight was given a little run, managing 11 starts that season, plus ten appearances as a sub.

His first full game was the one he mentioned – against Manchester United. 'That was on 29 December 1990,' says Rob Bishop. 'It was a 1–1 draw. Villa equalised with a Gary Pallister own goal after Steve Bruce had put United ahead with a penalty.'

What Dwight most remembers about it was what Tommy Docherty said about him afterwards. 'If that lad makes a First Division footballer, my name is Mao Tse-tung.'

Most football fans know this remark, as it has passed into folklore and is regularly quoted. What I personally was not sure about was where the Doc said it, or did he speak it, in some TV or radio commentary? Dwight of course was not sure. Just made a face when I mentioned it to him.

So, thank you Rob Bishop, once again. He dug out the exact quotation which appeared in 'The Doc's Casebook' in the *Sunday Mercury*, Birmingham, on 6 January 1991, a week after the Manchester United match. In his match

MAC'S STILL WORLD CLASS

PAUL McGRATH produced another first class performance for Aston Villa at Old Trafford last Saturday — and proved to me that he is still among the best defenders in the world.

Goalkeeper Nigel Spink received his share of the headlines for a string of superlative saves as Villa battled against the odds for a point, but it was McGrath who was the real star of the show.

Paul has been a tower of strength in the Villa defence since Graham Taylor resurrected his career.

His dodgy knees threatened to finish his playing days, but there's plenty of life in the old dog yet, and his former Old Trafford teammates would testify to that after another frustrating afternoon.

His cool-thinking and distribution of the ball whilst under pressure is a lesson which many young defenders should heed. He makes up for his loss of pace with a wonderful awareness.

United's jealous fans gave him some stick which I thought was unfair.

If Gary Pallister is worth £2.5 million then McGrath must be worth £10 million.

Apart from Paul's confident performance and Spink's acrobatics, I was very disappointed with Villa's uninspiring approach.

Tony Cascarino and Ian

THE DOC'S CASEBOOK

Ormondroyd look out of their depth up front. Villa don't play to Cascarino's strength.

They should play a conventional winger who can

● FRIGHTENED . . .
Dwight Yorke

pinpoint crosses on to Cascarino's head. If they are not prepared to change their game-plan to accommodate a winger, the Irish striker should be sold.

Likewise, Ormondroyd is a clumsy customer. You can almost hear his brain ticking when he gets hold of the ball. He's just not a natural footballer.

But it was new-boy Dwight Yorke who won the booby prize. If that lad makes a First Division footballer, my name is Mao Tse Tung.

He looks frightened every time he touches the ball.

His first instinct is to pass back instead of having the confidence to beat his defender.

report, he has a go at several players, as well as Dwight.

'Tony Cascarino and Ian Ormondroyd look out of their depth up front. Ormondroyd is a clumsy customer. You can almost hear his brain ticking when he gets hold of the ball. He's just not a natural footballer.

'But it was new boy Dwight Yorke who won the booby prize. If that lad makes a First Division footballer, my name is Mao Tse-tung.

'He looks frightened every time he touches the ball. His

first instinct is to pass back instead of having the confidence to beat his defender.'

Strong stuff to take, when you are still quite a tender flower, not yet blossoming. But Dr Venglos did play him another nine times that season. So he wasn't doing too badly.

'I was also very upset when Graham Taylor left,' says Tony Daley. 'He was a good manager. We all liked him. He was honest with you, though if you didn't pull your weight, he'd tell you so. But he had no favourites.

'When he left, I was probably more devastated than Dwight. I'd just signed a five-year contract.'

That's football, as footballers experience it. So what about Dr Jo?

'I liked Venglos. He was ahead of his time. He tried to introduce the sort of routines and systems which all clubs have, now that we have so many continental players and managers.

'He didn't ban alcohol or beer, but he told us that after a pint of beer, you should drink a pint of water. That would lessen the effects. The lads listened politely – but I don't think any did anything about it. Not at that time.

'He changed the training routines and got us into stretching before and after a match. Nobody had ever done stretching after a game before. He explained that soft muscles had to be eased into a game – and eased out of it. It's commonplace today, but not then. At the time, most us thought his ideas were a waste of time. Now we know he was right.'

Doug Ellis had appointed Jozef Venglos after meeting him at the World Cup in Italy in 1990. He was impressed by what he had done as coach for the Czech national team, getting them to third place in Euro 1980 and into the World Cup finals in 1982. He was also impressed by the fact that he spoke six languages and had a PhD from Bratislava University.

'The players were gob smacked by some of his modern methods of preparation,' remembers Doug Ellis.

'By his knowledge of all aspects of an athlete's requirements and by his courteous manner. The bottom line, however, was that it didn't work out, for whatever reason. By the end of December, we had won only four out of our opening 19 First Division games.

'Give him his due. He came to me about a month before the end of the season to say that if I was dissatisfied with his efforts, he would stand down voluntarily. That was something new, I can assure you.'

So technically it was not one of Doug's famous sackings. 'We parted amicably at the end of one season in the mutual knowledge that an idea that seemed a perfectly good one when undertaken had not been successful.'

So goodbye Dr Jo. Hello Big Ron.

19 *The trouble with any new manager when he comes in and doesn't know you is that he sticks with the older experienced players. I understand that. And if you haven't got a reputation either, well that's when things are hard.*

Dr Venglos did give me a few chances, but he needed results and quickly.

Then Ron Atkinson arrived. I don't think he ever really reckoned me. But I worked hard and I did have a couple of reasonable seasons under him. I became a regular in the first team, but I was never really sure of my place.

When my original two-year contract was up, Ron asked me to sign a new contract. So that was reassuring. It was for four years. Then I got a series of injuries.

The first happened in a pre-season tour of Japan in 1993. I was just warming up before a game. Lots of balls were flying around at me and I was lashing out, hitting them all, getting carried away, showing off, show-boating, I suppose.

Then I suddenly felt this pain in my thigh. Oh no, I thought, what have I done? I went and sat on the bench, hoping it would ease. It was my right thigh – and I'd ruptured it. I was injured and out of action, on and off, for six months. I hardly played that next season.

When I came back, Ron preferred to play his two more experienced strikers, Dalian Atkinson and Dean Saunders.

When Dalian also came back from an injury, he went straight back into the team. I was a bit upset about that. Then, when I did play, I tended to be used behind the front two, not as a striker.

The worst thing of all that happened to me, in my whole career so far, was the Coca-Cola Cup final in 1994.

I'd been in the team all the way through, and done well, so I thought, but on the day, Ron said he wasn't picking me. I was out. I couldn't believe it. I asked Ron why, but didn't get much of an answer. 'Just make sure that whenever Villa come back to Wembley, that you are in the team.'

I think he felt I didn't work hard enough, that was his real reason. I felt I did work hard. He didn't.

Villa won that game 3–1, beating Manchester United, so Ron's decision was proved right.

I did think of packing up, going back home to Tobago. But then I thought if I go back, I'll be a nobody. I've come here because I want to be somebody.

I had worked hard, so I thought. I hadn't drunk. I hadn't smoked. But it obviously wasn't enough. I was very upset.

Looking back, though, I think Ron did do me a favour. Though I hated him at the time. Because of him, after that I worked even harder.

Ugo Ehiogu, who joined Villa in July 1991, was given some special instructions by Ron Atkinson on how to handle Dwight.

'He told me in training that when Dwight turned his back on me, I had to punch him. I did it, a couple of times, but not too hard. He'd become a good friend by then. Ron thought that being punched would make him harder. I'm not sure Dwight agreed.'

Ugo became one of Dwight's closest friends at Villa. They share the same birthday, 3 November, but Ugo is a year younger. He was born in Hackney and became a trainee at West Brom, before joining Villa.

'I did see Dwight play before I arrived at Villa. He was probably only 18 and had come on as sub a couple of times. You could see he was rough around the edges, running around, not getting very far.

'In this match I watched, he went to shoot but his shot went miles wide. It was heading for the corner flag, but it ricocheted off someone – and went straight to Ian Olney who scored. Dwight went wild, as if it had been a deliberate pass. He was just so pleased to have had a hand in a goal.

'When I joined Villa, it was clear in training that he had bags of skill, but he needed toughening up, which was why Ron Atkinson told me to rough him up. Ron could be brutal. I suppose it could have destroyed some people.

'But Ron's methods didn't bother me. I'm strong. But Dwight liked to be told how good he was, to be comforted when things went wrong. Some players need that. Others just get on with it.'

However, Dwight's memory of his first two seasons with Ron were correct – he did do quite well, till the injuries. In the 1991–92 season he played 35 first team games, plus five as a sub. Then in the 1992–93 season, he played 27 games, with seven as a sub.

'The 1991–92 season was very important for Dwight,' says Rob Bishop.

'I'd gone with the team on a pre-season trip to Hanover when the news came out that Ron Atkinson had signed Dalian Atkinson from Real Sociedad for £1.6 million – a record for Villa at the time. Then he bought Cyrille Regis from Coventry. That meant there were now two senior players ahead of Dwight. He had suddenly gone right down the queue, having been slowly working his way up. Talking to him on the Hanover trip, I could tell how depressed he was.

'I later went to talk to Ron Atkinson, to write an article, and asked if it meant that Dwight did not figure in his plans any more. Ron said not at all – he had great faith in Dwight. I believed him and I later told Dwight what Ron had said to me. I think that cheered him up a bit.

'The best goal I saw Dwight score for Villa was during a home match against Forest in September 1991. He got the ball deep in his own half from Kevin Richardson, who was then the Villa captain. Dwight ran with the ball through their half, being chased by several Forest players. At the edge of their penalty area, he turned inside and chipped the ball over their goalie. It was breathtaking. I'm not sure if Dwight remembers that, but I always will.

'When I got home, after that Forest match, I got a call from Radio Trinidad. I thought it was just a private conversation, their reporter wanting to ask me things. I didn't realise at first I was live on air. They did that for quite a few weeks on a Saturday when Villa was at home. Till of course they managed to get in touch with Dwight himself and found out how to get him on the phone.

'I christened him the Calypso Kid after that. I'll send you a cutting, if you like.'

Which he kindly did.

It was dated 21 September 1991 and was an account of Villa's 3–1 win over Forest.

'The real gem in the Villa romp was Dwight Yorke, a lithe

and lively athlete whose potential is higher than the proposed new Witton Lane stand. The Calypso Kid had home fans drooling as he helped to create the first two goals and then conjured up a piece of Caribbean magic to leave defender Brett Williams on his backside and the ball floating tantalisingly over goalkeeper Mark Crossley.'

When Dwight signed his new contract, the headline on Rob Bishop's report in the paper was 'Calypso Kid Signs New 4 Year Deal'.

'In a match away to Grimsby, not long afterwards, I popped my head into Villa's dressing room afterwards. Dwight looked up at me and smiled, "Calypso Kid, eh?"'

Then of course came the injuries and Dwight's problems about getting back into the first team. This naturally worried his Mums. No, not Grace his real mum, whom he was ringing regularly, but Sheila, his landlady.

'We went to all his matches, from when he got in the first team,' says Sheila.

'"Come and watch me play, Mums," he'd say. "Good luck, love," I'd say to him. "Try and score." Oh yes, I saw every home match he played for Villa.

'I hadn't really been a big fan of football, till Dwight came along, though my dad always followed the Villa. Dwight had no family to support him, you see, not like all the other lads. I went to give him moral support.

'I could see he had talent, even from the beginning, but he was very laid back. Bigger lads would push him off the ball, "Push them back," I'd tell him.

'He did have some bad times. Oh he was very upset when Graham Taylor left. I think he really was on the verge of going back to Tobago. Such a shame. He'd hardly settled at the club when it happened.

'We do look upon him as our son, so we don't like to see him down-graded. When friends or other people in the village used to say "Dwight didn't do so well then in that game," we'd say "Who did?" We never blamed Dwight.

'He was weedy and thin when he arrived, so young and tender. He started doing body buildng early on. I remember him coming home, rolling up his sleeves and showing us his muscles. I could hardly see any difference, personally. So he went to the mirror to see if he himself could see any difference.'

'When he did that to me,' says Bryn, 'I said I've got more muscles in my tinkler than you've got on that arm ...'

'But he did stick at it,' says Sheila.

'Some of the older players, like David Platt and Gordon Cowans, they always stayed on after training to do work on their own in the gym. Dwight copied them. Most players of course rush straight home. Dwight did work on his chest and arm muscles and after 12 months you could see a big difference.

'He was on the team coach one day, coming home from some away match. He rang me, from the coach, to say "Mums, don't go to bed till I come home, please." I said, "What's the matter, love?" "I don't feel so well," he said.

'When he got in his eyes were running and he was obviously getting flu. He asked me to come up to his room. He had a bottle of this funny looking liniment I hadn't seen before. He'd brought it back with him from Tobago. Probably given to him by his mother. He asked me to rub it on his back. I was a bit embarrassed, and I didn't like the smell of it, but I gritted my teeth and did it. He did treat me as Mum, you see.

'Three days later, the worst of the flu had gone, but he was still not feeling so good. "Feel my skin," he kept saying. He's always worried about his skin, in case he gets any spots or anything, like all young lads, but this time he said he could feel some sort of pimples. I felt his skin and his hair – then I said, "Oh my God, I think you've got chicken pox." And he had. He went to the doctors and was off for two days.

'I can always tell when he's injured, even before the coaches can, just by the way he's running. And I can tell if he's upset by the shape of his body. He slaps his thighs.

'There was one time when I was watching him and I could sense there was something wrong "What's the matter with him?" I kept on thinking. He realised himself something was wrong, but no one could find out what it was. I thought it was his leg.

'And do you know what it was? Well, I don't know the technical terms, but it's something coloured people get. When they get bashed in a certain way, instead of just bruising, as a white person might do, it sets up something which starts to grow an extra bit of bone in its place. That was what was happening. He had an operation in the end, just a minor one. When I went to see him, this was in Little Aston Hospital, he held it up in a bottle for me to see, really pleased with himself.

'Have you looked closely at his skin? Oh it's really lovely. You know he never uses soap. He never washes his face. He just puts on baby cream, Johnson's Baby cream, or baby oil.

'He looks after his outside and his inside. That's the way they've been brought up. He's keen on taking cleansing stuff, outside and inside.'

Thanks for sharing, Sheila. All jolly interesting. Now back to football. What did you think of his Villa managers?

'Graham Taylor was a gentleman. We liked Venglos as well. He was very nice. But I never liked Ron Atkinson. Because of his treatment of Dwight of course.

'He was a bull at a gate, far too blunt and rough. Some lads need a bollocking sometimes, but not Dwight. He needs encouragement and kindness, then he'll blossom. If you tell him he looks nice or he played well, he'll be as pleased as punch. If you say he had a crap game, he'll get ever so upset.

'When Ron dropped him for the Coca-Cola Cup final, that was awful. So humiliating. Graham Fenton had been sent on loan to West Brom, then Ron Atkinson brought him back for the final in place of Dwight.

'Dwight was so depressed. I said, "Chin up, love, don't let them get you down. You've got to prove in the end that you're better. And you will. You've got more talent in your little finger than he has."

'When they won the Cup, and paraded it round the ground, Dwight was on the field. I noticed that he refused to touch it. I think he felt he hadn't taken part, so he shouldn't take any of the credit. It was all of course Ron Atkinson's fault.'

So what does Big Ron think? Another living legend in the exciting world of football.

I have to say that out of the 100 or so people I tried to contact for this book, then kept on contacting till I eventually made contact of some sort, Mr Atkinson was one of the few who actually rang me back. And that includes Dwight.

'Tell you my first memory of Dwight,' said Ron. 'He was responsible for one of the only mistakes I have ever made in a television commentary. I was doing Manchester City against Villa and when Dwight came on as sub, I said to Brian Moore that lad's called Mark Blake, he came on in the previous match ...

'When I did arrive at Villa, everyone told me he was a big talent. I had him in the first team from the beginning – in the first match against Sheffield Wednesday. I put him on the right wing and left out Tony Daley. We won 3–2. Dwight got a good goal that was disallowed.

'He was a regular in the team that season. I remember he got a hat trick against Shilton at Derby – and he missed two penalties.

'I normally played him on the right, to let Dalian Atkinson and Cyrille Regis go in the middle. I think he did well the next season as well.

'But then, yeah, he did get some injuries. One in Japan, I remember. It went again later. I think he was then out for another three months.

'When he came back, I had Atkinson and Dean Saunders up front. I thought they were the best pairing in the country at the time.

'I don't remember not rating him. That's not true. We weren't exactly flush with good strikers at the time.

'His problem was injuries and then of course when we played in Europe, I could only play three non-English players. That affected Bosnich as well. And the Irish lads.

'Yes, I do remember not playing him in that Coca-Cola Cup final. But to be fair, that was a very hard decision. You were only allowed two subs at that time. It was embarrassing having to decide. I left out big Ugo and Garry Parker and several others, who all expected to be in the team. To be fair, Dwight had not been a regular that season.

'I took a gamble bringing in Graham Fenton from the reserves for the final, which surprised some people. I was worried about Cantona, in Manchester United's midfield, wondering how to cope with him. I had seen Arsenal play 4–3–3 in a game against Manchester United They'd done well, so I thought I'd try it. It was an experiment for us, if you like, playing 4–3–3. I had Tony Daley and Atkinson on the wings, with Saunders up front in the middle. So I needed someone strong in midfield, to bolster it up. That's why I brought in Fenton, to play with Richardson and Townsend. It worked. Cantona was on fire at the time, but we contained him.

'Before the match, I got together the ones not picked, and told them in advance what I was doing. I told them all that next time, they had to make sure they were in the team.

'I remember Dwight as a smashing lad. No problems. I'm not surprised he's done so well. I brought in Dave Sexton to work on some of the younger players. Some of the tricks Dwight now uses, he learned them from Dave Sexton. People think they're natural, but Dave did work on him.'

Ron does seem to have a fairly rosy memory of his relationship with Dwight, which is not quite the same as Dwight's. Or some of the others'. So I asked him, as a generalisation, if it was fair to say that he was a manager who believed in bollockings?

'Oh if a lad does well, I'll give him credit. Definitely. But it is true I like people who are mentally strong. They're my sort of players. Dwight wasn't all that mentally strong at the time, so I suppose working with me, yeah, it was a learning curve for the lad.

'The happiest I ever saw him was when he was sitting in my office, with Bosnich. We were all watching the test match, the one when Brian Lara got the test match record, 365 or whatever.

'Yorkie was the most excited I'd ever seen him, jumping up and cheering. When Lara beat the record, he went wild.

'Dwight rang Lara on his mobile, while we were still watching the television. Garry Sobers had dropped on his knees. There was Lara, getting a call from Dwight, to congratulate him.

'Naturally, I opened a few bottles of champagne ...'

Big Ron survived as manager till November 1994, though by that time chairman Doug Ellis was going off him. In his book, Doug Ellis says that Ron had started to favour certain players, such as Dalian Atkinson, who was allowed to get away with back chat to Ron, which others would not dare.

'I was also more likely to see Ron on television, explaining where other teams were going wrong, than sit over a quiet drink with him and talk about Aston Villa's failings.'

It was a defeat, 4–3 by Wimbledon on 9 November, after Villa had been 3–1 up, which did it, leaving them very near the bottom of the league. Deadly Doug struck, and another Villa manager was on his way.

21 *After Ron left, Brian Little arrived. That was when my career really took off. Brian was young and open to new ideas and new people.*

I found that he had been watching me long before he became the Villa manager. You never know in football who is watching you. So when he arrived, he said the number 9 position can be yours. It was up to me, to take it or leave it, but he would give me a good run. That's all you can ever ask as a player.

And he did give me a good run. Because of that, he instilled confidence in me, and I played better. Brian Little is my sort of manager. I felt I could always talk to him. So I'll always be grateful to him.

By 1995, I felt at last sure of my place. I didn't have to worry any more if I was going to be sub or not. It was great being able to walk into the dressing room and know I was playing.

It had taken a long time, almost five years, and had been a struggle, what with the injuries and changes of manager. There were times when I thought it might be best to move on, when you see players coming in for big money. But I'd been prepared to work at it, knowing I would eventually get my chance.

In that 1994-95 season, with Brian in charge, I finally felt at home in Birmingham. I felt accepted.

I became top scorer, and started to win Carling Player of the Month awards.

One of the problems with this was when I got called up to play for the Trinidad and Tobago team. It always left me in a dilemma. I know people out there were not pleased with me, and I have been criticised, but I don't think they really understood the position I was in.

I had turned up and played, many times, even when once I got injured against Jamaica and came back unable to play. I was stuck alone at home, on my own, with my injury. Nobody from Trinidad even rang up to ask how I was.

But later, when I did become a regular in the Villa team, what was I going to do? I'd fought and struggled so long to get my place, but if I got injured playing for Trinidad, I might lose it again. Or they might buy someone.

It's a long tiring journey to get out there and, with due respect, Trinidad and Tobago were not always playing vital or big matches. Then sometimes, against smaller countries, there would be people on the other side who just wanted to kick me, because I was a so-called star from England.

In December 1995, Trinidad and Tobago called me up to play in the Gold Cup, an international tournament in the USA. It would have meant missing four big matches for Villa – the FA Cup third round, the Coca-Cola quarter finals and two league matches, one against Manchester United and one against Spurs.

I didn't want to get on the wrong side of my country, as I love my country, but I didn't want to miss those Villa games. They were the ones paying me. It was a terrible decision. I said no in the end. But it was very hard. People back home didn't really understand, didn't put themselves in my shoes. When I tried to explain, I could never get everyone out there to understand. Still can't, really. I still get asked about it.

In 1996, we won the Coca-Cola Cup again – and this time I was in the team. In July 1996, after that win, I signed another four-year contract with Villa. I was very happy with them, with the chairman and with Brian. They both told me the direction they wanted to take the club and I was very enthusiastic.

My agent did all the details, looked after the new contract. Oh yeah, I had an agent for some time. Tony Stephens. He's done a hell of a lot for my career.

I'd bought my own house by then, moved out of Sheila's after almost three years. I think I paid £95,000 for the first one. Then I moved to a bigger one, which cost £200,000. I wanted my own place, where I could bring my mother over, so she could stay with me. And entertain my friends ...

22 Sheila was very upset when Dwight left home, or at least her home, the one he had lived in for two and a half years.

'He told Bryn first, not me. When I was told, I cried for a month. He said he wanted to buy his own house, but he would still look upon me as his Mums. He wanted me still to look after him.

'I thought he was too young to be on his own in his house, but that was because I didn't want him to leave. I thought of all the temptations. When he stayed here, all he did was eat and sleep. That's all young footballers need after all. He'd often go to bed in the afternoon, after training, and I'd have to wake him up at 7.00, so he'd come down and watch TV. This is an ideal village for a young player. No night life, nowhere to go.

'It's true he didn't drink till his 21st birthday. It was going to be in a restaurant, then Doug Ellis said he could have it at the club, in the McGregor suite. There were about 150 there. All the Villa players were trying to get Dwight drunk, buying him rounds. Yes, you had to pay for your drink. He had the last dance with me, by which time he was getting on a bit and had his arms round me. I was holding him up by then. As I did so, I thought of all the girls who would like to be in my position ...

'But he never drank, all the time he was living here. Nor took any drugs. We used to discuss drugs, round the table, and he'd say he'd heard of some really nice people who used drugs and I said don't believe it, and don't try it. And don't go boozing. Look at George Best, I said. I used to tell him if he started drinking, and was out somewhere, it would be very easy for someone to slip an Ecstasy tablet in his drink. Oh I know all about those tricks.

'When he did start drinking, he didn't drink much. He's like me. One can go to his head. I remember being in the players' lounge at Villa with him, after a bad result, and he ordered a double Bailey's and ice. I've got to have a drink, he said. No, you don't, I said. One bad game, but think of all the good games you've had. By the next game, you'll have forgotten this game. Brian Small's mother heard what I was saying, so when Dwight wasn't looking, she knocked back half of his drink. He never realised.

'Players can be so gullible, thinking drink will cheer them up. They don't realise their so-called friends are always trying to get them drunk. Paul McGrath was off the drink at one time, thanks to his wife, but behind her back, people were lining up drinks for him.

'So you can see why I was worried about him buying a house. The club thought he was ready. Ron said it was a good way to invest.

'So he bought this three-bedroom house at Walmley, about 20 minutes' drive away. Quite a nice area. Villa own a few houses there, where they put up foreign players who have just arrived.

'I went to look at it with him and I hated the woman who was selling it. Not because of her. Just because she was selling it to Dwight. Dwight asked me to help him buy his furniture. I liked that, being able to spend someone else's money.

'He'd been told by the club to buy a really firm mattress. Orthopaedic, I think it's called. It seemed fine enough, till I heard the price. Six thousand pounds! Ridiculous. I wouldn't let him get it. In the end he got one for £2,000 which was expensive enough. We chose his three-piece suite together. I was pleased he chose colours I liked – pastel shades.

'I kept an eye on his bills. Workmen think they are on a soft touch, when they come across people like Dwight.

'I went over twice a week, Tuesdays and Fridays, to clean his house, do his washing and ironing. He just lived there alone, though there was often a friend staying or relations from Tobago. He can cook a bit, in fact he did take some cooking lessons, but mainly he sends out for food. Or he goes to a Chinese. He loves Chinese food.

'He'd only been in his new house a few weeks when I got a call from a neighbour, saying there was water coming from an overflow. He was away that evening, playing at Arsenal. I was just about to drive over, when he rang me. He'd just got in, switched the lights on – and they all fused. Then he found the place full of water. There were ceilings down, carpets ruined, walls damaged. Oh it cost thousands to put it right. Apart from that, he did manage better than I expected.

'But I always worried when they'd had a bad game. I thought poor lad, he'll be coming home to an empty house, feeling upset, with no one to talk to.

'After about two years, he moved to a much bigger house, when he was getting more money. It was really because he had too many clothes. Honestly. I counted his shoes when he moved – and he had 82 pairs. I didn't count the suits, but he must have had 50.'

One reason why Dwight was now in the money, able to afford expensive houses and clothes, was the arrival in his life of Tony Stephens, who became Dwight's agent in 1991.

Tony is 51 and was born in Birmingham. He worked in an accountant's office on leaving school, but didn't finish his studies, deciding it was not for him. He went into marketing and in 1982 was appointed commercial manager of Aston Villa. After four years he moved to Wembley as Sales and Marketing Director.

In 1988 he set up on his own, working from his home in the West Midlands, calling himself TSA – Tony Stephens Associates – specialising in sports marketing.

The first footballer he handled personally was David Platt who had just arived at Villa from Crewe, in February 1988, aged 21. Platt had been a late starter, taken on as a boy at Manchester United then released before he had ever played a game for them. He went to Crewe, then in Division

Four, where he stayed for three seasons before being bought by Villa for £150,000.

'I was working at the time on the launch of a new football boot and the company wanted someone young, sensible, not too well known, but with a good future who played for one of the Midlands clubs. I don't consider myself a judge of a footballer. But I've always said that 'knowledge is knowing or knowing where knowledge is.' So I asked around, and all of them mentioned David Platt. I'd not been aware of him. I met him and he did the boot deal and it all went well. He struck me as a very intelligent, sensible young man. I got him quite a lot of promotional and sponsorship work. Gradually, I started looking after all his off-the-pitch activities.'

Tony's income came and still comes primarily from his clients' off-the-field commercial activities. There is nothing in it for him when they move or demand a wage increase.

'The first time I was aware of Dwight was in early 1991. We were in negotiations with Bari in Italy for David Platt's transfer. The deal was £5.5 million, the biggest British transfer record at that time. The press had got inklings of it, but nothing had been signed and sealed.

'David had returned from a trip to Italy, but we were keeping details out of the media. David suggested Dwight as part of the escape plot. It all happened at the training ground. David's car was parked in the car park, so the press were hanging around it, waiting to catch him.

'Dwight had moved his own car up, right outside the main building. He comes waltzing out, smiling away as usual, all laid back, carrying his training kit. He walks to his car and stands beside it, smiling, talking to the press.

'David has been watching inside, waiting for Dwight to get into his car. He then dashes out, running like mad for Dwight's car, not his own, as the press expected. He gets to Dwight's car – but Dwight has been so busy smiling and chatting he's forgotten to unlock it. So the press push across and trap David beside Dwight's car while Dwight fumbles and messes around trying to open it. Eventually he does and drives David away.

'That incident still makes me smile. I saw it on television. The local TV company were there, covering the story. I love seeing the look on the journalists' faces when they realise David is not going in his own car ...

'The thing about David Platt is that from the moment I took him on, he was totally reliable. If I said he had to be at the Birmingham International Exhibition Centre, Hall 5, at a certain time, to meet the managing director of XY and Z company, David would always be there – five minutes early.

'In the early days with Dwight, well, he was pretty hopeless. He would turn up at the wrong place on the wrong day. He was such a lovely lad, though, that you couldn't hold it against him. Over the years, he's got much better and is very reliable.

'I took him on after David Platt raved about him, said he was the best young talent at the club, the most talented young player he had seen.

'When I take anyone on, I always think in the long term. I try to outline a scenario for the next ten years – where they'll be, what they might be earning, if all goes well. I can't remember precisely what I told Dwight. At the time he was only making occasional appearances in the first team. I estimated by his mid-20s he would be a regular, then would go abroad, as David Platt had done. That was the thinking in 1991. The Italian clubs had all the money and the best players. It also seemed to me that Dwight's talents were more Italian, that it would suit him there, and he would do well.

'The first commercial contract I got for him was for a new sort of football – a soft-case ball called Skillball. It was a very good idea – a ball for young kids which was between a plastic ball and a real football. The press launch was at Highbury, so we all went down there. It was arranged that Dwight would show off the ball, demonstrate his skills, have a kick-around with a few kids on Arsenal's astroturf training pitch. Then he would meet the press and the commercial and marketing people, have a few drinks with them.

'It was only at the end of the drinks stage that I realised I hadn't seen Dwight for about an hour. I went to find him – and he was still having a kick-around with the kids.

'He does have amazing juggling skill. Someone told me about when he was a boy in Tobago, when he had no boots. He went into this sports shop one day and said to the shop owner if he kept the ball up in the air with his head 100 times, would he give him a free pair of boots. The man said yes. Dwight did it, there and then in the shop, amongst all the clutter. The man said that was too easy. He wouldn't give him the boots after all. Dwight then said he'd make it harder. There was a rubbish bin in the shop. Dwight said if he did the 100 headers while standing in the bin, would he give him the boots. The man said yes. Dwight did it and finally got the boots. I love that story ...

'Dwight did have some setbacks early on, when Ron put him back into the reserves. He found solace with Cyrille Regis, a senior player at Villa at the time. Cyrille has a saying that when you first emerge as a professional, and get into the first team, you are not a true professional. It's only when you get the first knocks and setbacks, and come back from them, that's when you can truly consider yourself a professional.

'Ron Atkinson did specialise in giving players mental strength. I think it was true in Dwight's early career that he needed to be toughened up, in every sense. When he lost the ball you would see his arms flapping by his side. Soon he could tear apart the toughest defence. It's remarkable how he improved.

'But of course his injuries held him back. I went to see him in hospital after he had been knocked unconscious in a match. It was frightening. He looked like something out of *Silence of the Lambs*. He was being cheerful, but I remember it striking me how he was alone in this country, with his family half way round the world. You tend to forget that, till something like that happens and you don't have the normal family support system.'

Sheila of course saw herself as his surrogate family and was appalled by this particular accident.

'It was a home match against Coventry, one of the few I ever missed. Bryn was off work ill and I had to stay at home. I was listening to the match on the radio, then a visitor called and I switched off for a while. When they'd gone, I switched on again and I couldn't hear Dwight's name being mentioned. After it was over, Brian Little was being interviewed and he said Dwight had a broken nose. Oh, I burst into tears. Bryn on crutches, and now Dwight injured. It was December 1995. Must have been. As I was listening, I'd been putting up our Christmas decorations.

'There was a call from the hospital, the Priory in Birmingham, ringing me, as next of kin, to tell me Dwight was being taken for a brain scan. I asked if he wanted me to come in, and they said no, just relax. Come in tomorrow, after the operation.

'I went in next morning and oh, what a sight, such a sad little boy. His eyes were all swollen and he had this face mask on which made him look so weird, like something in a horror film. He had things up his nose and tubes everywhere. You just wanted to hug him, this sad little boy, all on his own, in a strange country.

'The player who crashed into him and knocked him out, David Busst of Coventry, later broke his own leg and had to retire from the game early. When you think of that, you realise that Dwight has been lucky on the whole with injuries.'

'Brian Little was very understanding with Dwight,' says Tony Stephens. 'He himself was injured at 26 and went out of the game, which was a great loss to Villa and to himself. He sold cars for a time, and insurance, and was drifting away from football, till he came back as a coach. From his arrival, he could see Dwight's potential which others had perhaps missed. He knew how to deal with him, encourage him. I think having been a striker himself also helped.'

But as with so many managers, at Villa and elsewhere, Brian Little's powers of motivation and management skills began to fade. While many players had been scared of Ron Atkinson, or at least frightened of his sharp tongue, several began to take liberties with Brian Little. Slowly he began to lose control of his players, and himself, appearing mentally exhausted and confused. Doug Ellis was worried that his confidence had taken a battering and that he had been affected by his children being bad-mouthed at school. In February 1998, Brian Little resigned and was replaced by John Gregory.

Dwight had been happy enough under Brian Little, when things were going well, but now he began to think he might have made a mistake by signing that four-year contract in 1996.

'During 1998,' says Tony Stephens, 'there were rumours that Sampdoria, Athletico Madrid as well as Manchester United were after him, but nothing came of it.

'He had two years left on his contract. We discussed it at the beginning of the 1998-99 season. He felt he would like to move to a bigger club, and have a chance of winning something, but as nothing had happened, he just had to knuckle down and get on with it.'

'He told me in about early 1998 that he'd heard two clubs were after him,' says Sheila.

'Juventus and Manchester United. We used to sit and discuss what he would choose, if both came for him.

'I used to say I'd rather he was at Manchester United – not just for personal reasons, as he would be nearer, but I reckoned that as a single man, he should be in England, where he now had so many friends. If you were courting, had a partner or a wife, that would be different. You wouldn't be so lonely then. So you could move anywhere. That's what I think.

'Anyway, nothing came of it. It was just newspaper gossip. But he began to say he'd like a move, in order to win something. I've got no silver in the cupboard, he used to say.

'Money didn't come into it. Football comes first with him, and second and third. Money or women or anything else, they don't really matter.'

There had been numerous rumours all summer. I was quite delighted with them, but I wasn't sure what they meant. I hadn't been told anything. Just what I'd read or heard. As the new season began [1998–99], yeah, it was a bit unsettling.

The first match of the season was against Everton and I know people said I played poorly, because I wanted to leave. But it wasn't true. Nobody played well in that match. John Gregory was quoted as saying that my heart was not involved. That really hurt.

I had given nine years to Villa, given everything to the team. For the last few years, I had been the team's inspiration. So I was so upset to be accused of not trying. It was as if he was trying to make me a scapegoat, to blame me for whatever might happen.

It is true I was disappointed when Brian Little had been pushed out. Then Grego had me playing behind Stan [Collymore] and Savo [Milosevic]. I don't like playing in the middle. I don't think it suits my temperament. I like to play forward. But I had agreed with Grego. I thought it might work. I was willing to try it. But it hadn't worked, not really.

After nine years, without actually winning much, the thought of going to a club like Manchester United was my dream. It was what I'd come into football for – to get to the very top. So of course, yes, I was thrilled at the idea of Manchester United being interested in me.

The transfer deadline for Europe was Thursday, 20 August – that's if you wanted to play in Europe for a new club. The day before, nothing had happened. I had still been told nothing, but the papers were full of stories.

Villa apparently wanted £16 million for me, but Manchester United were only prepared to offer £10 million. That's what was being written. Six million is a huge difference. I couldn't see them agreeing. So it seemed all off. I was pretty depressed.

I went to Tony's office and David Platt was there. He has been around a lot, so I was a bit cheered when he said that all transfers need a bit of luck. All the same, there seemed no time left for luck to happen, with only a few hours to go.

That evening, after I left Tony's office, I went to play golf at the Belfry. I played with Mick Maloney, the managing director of the Belfry. Funnily enough, he's a big Manchester United fan. I told him that I thought I wouldn't be going. It was too late now.

I can't remember the score, but he beat me, by a little. I haven't got an official handicap. It goes up and down but I'd say I was generally about a ten.

At 9.00, I came home and had something to eat. Various people rang, including Tony, still saying it might or might not be on. I was still being kept in the dark, but he'd ring me if he heard anything. It seemed clear that the problem was the fee. They'd obviously got stuck on that.

At 10.30, Brian Little rang me on my mobile. 'I might have done you a big favour,' he said. Martin Edwards had rung him to talk about me, what I was like to handle. He'd given me a good recommendation. I suppose when a club is signing any player, they ring round managers who have worked with them.

I knew then something was happening. It gave me a bit of hope. But I went to bed feeling very tense and nervous. So near, yet still so far.

When I got up the next morning, I still had not heard anything officially. So once again I thought that's it. It's all off. It hasn't *happened and it won't now. I'll just have to go to training and carry on as normal. I'll be remaining a Villa player ...*

24 Oh, what tangled webs transfers are. Before, during and afterwards, there are so many trails, so many rumours, so many theories, so many trivialities, not all of which are remembered, long after it's all signed and sealed and in the record books. Even the leading players, the main participants, don't see the whole picture. Not at the time. Afterwards, they often forget, or prefer to forget, things they said or thought or considered important or significant at the time.

'At the start of that season,' says Tony Stephens, 'I have to admit he did have a poor match. Against Everton he didn't play as well as usual. Some fans thought he was just doing it. I knew he wasn't, but all transfer talk had clearly unsettled him.

'I knew nothing about Manchester United's interest, except that if they wanted him for Europe, it was now almost too late. They'd need to sign him by 5.00 on the Thursday. I thought it couldn't possibly happen now.

'He came to my office mid-afternoon on the Wednesday. David Platt was there and also Robbie Keane, a young player at Wolves I had just taken on.

'Dwight's body language gave away how he felt – all sloping shoulders, very flat, very low. We sat around having coffee and he brightened up a bit as we all talked. We did talk about transfers, because of course David has been through so many – Crewe, Villa, Bari, Juventus, Sampdoria, Arsenal. In all, he has been sold for over £22 million. He told Dwight that the most important thing with any transfer is luck.

'As we sat and talked, the *Birmingham Evening Mail* arrived. They had done a readers' poll about Dwight. There had been talk for weeks about him leaving the club and the fans were getting fed up, saying he was deliberately trying to get away by playing badly. Which wasn't true. The poll showed that 80 per cent of the supporters thought Dwight should go. I was staggered by this, that the fans had swung round so much. They had loved him the previous season, now they were all against him.

'I faxed the poll to Martin Edwards at Manchester United. I still don't know how much that affected what later happened.

'I suspect that Doug Ellis, chairman of Villa, also saw the same poll. I don't know what approaches had been made at that stage, or what discussions had happened. Dwight had been told nothing. Neither had I.

'I suspected that if Doug Ellis did read that poll, and had been thinking of letting Dwight go, that might have convinced him.

'Earlier on, when everyone loved Dwight, there would have been a riot, if they had sold him. No chairman wants to make an unpopular decision. But now the fans had turned against him.'

So did that newspaper poll make a difference to Doug Ellis's attitude? When I asked him about his memory of that transfer, he told me first about a visit by Dwight, which Dwight himself had never mentioned.

'There had been offers for Dwight, so I knew people wanted him, but I said no, certainly not, he's not for sale. I had told Dwight myself. Sorry, son, you're not going anywhere. You've signed for another two years. That's it. You've got to accept it.

'Every time anyone asked me, or anyone else at the club, we said the same. We're not selling Dwight Yorke.'

On Wednesday, the day before the transfer deadline, Doug Ellis was at home at Four Oaks, on the private estate near Sutton Coldfield where he lives. He happened to look out into his drive, around 7.45 in the morning.

'I saw a BMW which I recognised and knew straight away it was Dwight. I went down and he said he was unable to sleep at nights, because of the transfer speculation. He begged me to let him go. I said sorry, son. No chance.

'He said he'd given the club nine years of service, surely that showed he was loyal. I said yes, but we gave you your chance in the first place.

'We talked for about half an hour and I repeated that he wasn't going. And I meant it. He was in a sad state. Almost sobbing. Least that's how it seemed to me.

'He said he would have to accept it, but he intimated he wouldn't be in the best frame of mind, sitting out the next two years. I can't remember his words exactly. But that's the impression I got. No it wasn't a threat. It was just that it would be hard for him, not being able to go to Manchester United.

'Again I said, sorry, son, we love you too much here. But that's final. I went to put my arm round his shoulder as he left, but he dodged me. He might have muttered something under his breath. I didn't hear exactly. Perhaps even that he wouldn't speak to me again. I said as far as I was concerned, he would always be my son. That's how we parted. With me saying sorry, no chance ...

'But after he'd gone, I started thinking. I definitely had no intention of releasing him. I felt if we ever did, the fans would slaughter me. We also didn't need the money. Oh no. That wasn't a factor. We'd rather have had Dwight than the money.

'But he had looked so sad. I am at heart a softie. His appearance had touched me. He's still so young, I thought. Perhaps we should give him his chance to progress further. Why keep him when he's so unhappy?

'When I got to the club I talked to two of my colleagues and told them what I thought. We then had an executive board meeting, along with John Gregory. Oh we never do such things without the agreement of the manager ...'

So what did John Gregory think. And what had he thought, during this saga?

John had returned to the club as manager in February 1998, but had been there earlier, as reserve team manager, under Brian Little. So he knew Dwight well. 'When I came back, he was our star, our number one player. Everyone talked about him, everyone sang about him on the terraces. "Dwight Yorke, Dwight Yorke".'

John sang me the song, just in case I didn't know it, but then John loves singing and is a keen follower of popular music.

'A great player, and a great trainer, always the last to leave training, and very popular. A great mixer in the dress-ing-room, though he could be a bit moody.'

How do you mean?

'Well, if all was not right in his world, he could get a bit low. I put it down to being a single man, not having some-one at home to discuss his problems with. I would see him going off to his big house, knowing he was going home to be alone. But then he chose that life. I think he is a bit of a loner, really.

'Anyway, from the moment I arrived in February, he was outstanding. We won nine of the last 11 matches of the season, and he was outstanding. That chipped penalty against Seaman of Arsenal in the last game was wonder-ful.

'I think it was probably during those performances, at the end of the season, that Manchester United targeted him. There were noises. I knew that if they did come along, I would have to deny him the chance to go to a big club.

'In that match against Everton, at the start of the next season, he played with his head stuck up his arse. I am not saying he did it deliberately. He was there, but his mind wasn't there.

'I didn't want him to go. My chairman said if you don't want him to go, we won't let him go. We did offer him more money, more than Manchester United went on to offer him. But when I looked into his eyes, I knew it would be hard. I knew what we'd face over the next three months, if we didn't let him go. It would take that time, just to settle him down again. Then the season would be over – with only one season left on his contract. He'd never sign another for Villa. He'd leave us, and we'd get nothing. While we would have denied him his big chance. Yeah, it was difficult, but I still wanted to keep him.

'Then what hurt me was a quote in the *Evening Mail*, on the Tuesday I think it was. Dwight was quoted as saying he didn't want to play for Villa again. That hurt me, more than his poor game against Everton. It hurt the shirt. That's what I knew the fans would think.

'During the Wednesday, Deadly contacted me about a meeting, but I had to go out first with a friend from Scotland who was visiting me. We went out to a restaurant. I took my mobile with me into the restaurant, which I never do. Never. It was because Alex [Ferguson] was going to ring me.

'During the meal, it did ring, and I went outside to take it. When I came back, there were two Villa fans at the next table.

' "Is it good news?" said one of them. I said it could be.

' "He's not staying, is he?"

'Now that surprised me, their attitude. They clearly didn't want him to stay. It stuck in the back of my mind, made me realise the fans had turned against him.

'I then went to Deadly's for the meeting, about ten. I like to think it was my decision, that it was left to me. I weighed up all the arguments. Most of all I thought shit, keeping him is not going to solve it. It's not going to go away, so we might as well take the money. By 11.30, we had agreed to accept £12 million. They'd started at £8 million.

It was me that said £16 million – which I believed he was worth. It wasn't a bad return, was it, for what we paid for him.'

'Yes, John agreed 100 per cent with me,' says Doug Ellis. 'I knew he had been critical of the way Dwight had been performing.'

What about the newspaper poll, had that been a factor? Neither Doug Ellis nor John Gregory was aware of the poll.

'My motives were pure sympathy for Dwight,' says Doug. 'When I saw his mouth dropping that morning, I felt so sorry for him. I had always known him with a smile on his face.'

When I told Dwight about his early morning meeting, pleading with Doug Ellis, he said, oh yeah, he'd forgotten that. But Doug's memory was also at fault, he said. He was driving a Mercedes that day. Not a BMW.

It had clearly been an emotional time for him, when he felt depressed and vulnerable, not to say desperate, rather than his normal public, smiley cheerful self.

He also hadn't told me that one of the people he rang was Graham Taylor, his old mentor.

'He'd often kept in touch, after I left Villa,' says Graham. 'During times when he was feeling down or unhappy. With no disrespect to Villa, I said Manchester United was the sort of club he should go to. The chances are they'll be in Europe every year, probably the only English club you can bank on, at present. If he got the chance, he had to go.'

But of course when Dwight woke up, on the transfer day, he still hadn't heard anything officially, didn't know about Mr Ellis's or John Gregory's late-night change of heart. He still had to drag himself off to training ...

Just before I left for training, I got a call from Fergie. 'Congratulations,' he said. 'You could be joining us today.'

I rang Tony straight away. He said keep the line clear. We could hear something soon, but they're still haggling.

At 9.30, nothing had happened. I began to think again that it was all off, as there were now only a few hours to go. I was still a Villa player. So I had to go training, didn't I?

I rang Tony again and he said yes, go to training, but pack a suit in the car, just in case.

I arrived a bit late for training, at 10.30, which wasn't like me, but nobody said anything. I sat in the dressing room, taking off my tracksuit for training, feeling sad and fed up.

Some of the lads, like Ian Taylor and Mark Draper, made funny remarks. 'Oooh, he's not going anywhere, is he?' You have to take that sort of thing. 'Oooh, Dwight's not very happy, is he?'

I was very upset that it didn't seem to be happening, but I just sat there, trying to look cool.

Steve Harrison, the first team coach, was getting ready for the training session. He's a great bloke, great joker with a great sense of humour. He had two bits of paper in his hand. 'On one bit of paper it's got Dwight Yorke's name – and the other bit of paper hasn't. I dunno what's going on ...'

Out in the corridor there's a telephone, near the coaches' room. I heard it ringing and one of the apprentices answered it. I can't remember which one it was now. I could hear him answering it and then he came into the dressing room.

'Dwight,' he said, 'there's a Tony Stephens on the phone for you.' I'm sure he didn't know who Tony was. I went to the phone, as casually as possible.

'Congratulations,' says Tony. 'Get your boots and say your goodbyes ...'

I went slowly back into the dressing room. I sat silently for one minute, taking a deep breath. I tried to look sad, so they'd think it was bad news, that the deal was off. Then I started to put my tracksuit on again – and they all knew I was going. I had a big cheeky smile on my face by then.

I shook hands with every player, all the apprentices, every one, and the coaching staff, the tea ladies, the chefs.

Most of them said the same – 'You spawny begger.'

Spawny? I suppose it's a Brummie expression. I'd picked it up at Villa. It just means lucky, I think.

My particular friends like Mark [Bosnich] and Ugo [Ehiogu] said things like 'Can you put in a good word for us.'

They were all very good, very happy for me. Nobody said anything nasty. No, I couldn't sense anyone hating me for going. I was sad to go, in a way, as I'd had nine happy years at Villa. I'd trained, travelled, eaten with them for so long. It did seem strange, to be going away.

I went into Grego's office. I said we hadn't seen eye to eye in the last few weeks, we'd had our difficulties, but I said I'd just like to thank him for accepting it, that I was now going.

He gave me a big hug and a cuddle. And he meant it. He was wishing me good luck, being really decent.

So when I read later that he'd said those words – 'If I had a gun I'd shoot Dwight Yorke' – I couldn't believe it. I was so surprised, after he had hugged me. I thought it was terrible.

I took it that he thought I'd somehow acted badly, nastily. Otherwise why would he want to shoot me? I'd done nothing wrong. I didn't start it all. I didn't ask for a transfer. I didn't do anything. It was all fixed by the two clubs, between themselves. They made the decision. Not me.

Yes, I was also upset by the fans turning against me. That's the world we live in today. But I was more upset by Grego's remark, about wanting to shoot me, than the Villa poll.

26 What a lot of hurt there can be in football. Grown men crying on the pitch, or getting upset off it. I suppose that has to be expected, now that they all kiss and cuddle each other whenever something really good or exciting, or just vaguely emotional happens.

All that upset John Gregory, so he says, was Dwight's remark in the newspaper about wanting to leave Villa.

'That did hurt, but I never fell out with him personally. Yes, I did give him a cuddle on the morning he left. I was pleased for him, if not for me.

'When I said I wanted to take a gun and shoot him, I was thinking of it being like losing a lover or a wife. You've been together, all been wonderful, then someone else comes along, she says she's leaving you, and you think, if I can't have her, no one else will. That's why I thought of shooting him. That's all it meant. He was our most influential player – and now we were losing him. He was going off to Manchester, and leaving us ...'

It wasn't of course all signed and sealed, not at that stage. Things can always go wrong, especially when it has to be done in a hurry, at the last minute.

'It wasn't till 10.15 on the Thursday morning,' says Tony Stephens, 'that we heard Manchester United had made an offer and Villa had accepted it. But it was still subject to a medical and Dwight agreeing personal terms. Manchester United made it clear that everything would have to be agreed and in place and all signed by five that evening, or the deal was off.

'When I phoned Dwight at the ground, I told him to get his medical records and I'd pick him up in 45 minutes. At 11.15, we were in my Jaguar driving up the M6 to Manchester.

'The traffic was terrible. It seemed to take for ever, yet every minute mattered. No one at this stage knew anything

115

about it, outside the Manchester United and Villa chairmen and main officials.

'While we were driving, Dwight rang his mother in Tobago. He said he was joining Manchester United and sounded very excited. He was jumping the gun, of course. It might not yet happen, but I couldn't stop him. I don't think his mother really took it in.

'Initially, all the transfer talk had not bothered Dwight. But then he'd begun to realise that at the age of 26, this was a once-in-a-lifetime chance. Playing for Trinidad and Tobago, with due respect, isn't going to get you world recognition.

'And Aston Villa, though a good Premier club, has not got the European and world stature of Manchester United. So Dwight had now set his heart on it.

'But I knew if it didn't happen today, it was definitely off. Manchester United would draw out. Then who knows if they'd ever come back, or what would happen to Dwight in the season ahead.

'While Dwight went for his medical, I went in to see the details of the contact they were offering.

'Only three weeks earlier, I had been there to arrange a five-year extension to David Beckham's contract.'

Tony Stephens does happen to have a rather choice portfolio of players. Tony might have been lucky to have found Dwight when Dwight was young and unknown, thanks to his relationship with David Platt, but Dwight was equally fortunate to find himself being managed by a highly respected agent with about the best group of players in England at that time – including Alan Shearer, the current captain, and Michael Owen, still the boy wonder. As well as a Master Beckham.

It meant that when things had to be done quickly, Tony already knew his way round Old Trafford, physically and professionally. He knew the officials likely to be involved and knew the sort of clauses not to request, as Manchester United would find them unacceptable.

'I'd just started to go through the contract and I got a call from Dwight. He'd left his medical records in the boot of my car. So that was a bit of a panic, getting them over to him.

'At 4.30, Dwight was back, having passed his medical. That side was all in order.

'We already knew that Villa had offered him more money to stay. A club like Villa, which might only have a few stars, can usually improve offers, even if it means upsetting their wage structure, in order to keep their special players. At Manchester United, where they have so many stars, their wage salary is rigid. No one breaks it.

'I knew all that, so we didn't argue much on the money side.

'Dwight had not started the transfer talk. It had begun with Manchester United's offer, but all round, it was the best time for it.

'With only two years left on his Villa contract, under the Bosman rule, Dwight would have been free to go anywhere in the world – and Villa would not have got a penny. This is one of the many reasons why players today have such power, and can earn such huge amounts. When an out-of-contract player signs for a new club, he can demand an enormous salary because the club doesn't have to pay a transfer fee.

'So it was a good deal for Villa, in the financial sense. If Dwight had stayed any longer, his price would have collapsed. To keep him for another two years, probably paying him around a million a year in salary and bonuses, then losing him in the end for nothing, would have meant over two years they would have notionally lost £14 million.

'It was also a good, if expensive, deal for Manchester United. Alex Ferguson had realised his team had to be strengthened if they wanted to progress in Europe this season.

'The transfer fee came to £12.6 million – that included the League levy of 5 per cent. It was a record for

Manchester United, and the second highest British transfer fee.'

The highest was of course Newcastle United's purchase of Alan Shearer from Blackburn Rovers for £15 million. Another of Tony's boys.

The background to the transfer from Manchester United's point of view was later made clearer, thanks to Alex Ferguson's autobiography, *Managing My Life*, published by Hodder in August 1999.

The delays were partly explained by Ferguson, surprisingly, feeling under threat at the time, after the chairman of Manchester United plc, Sir Roland Smith, had asked him if he felt like calling it a day. Then he had the problem of a tight budget, having already spent what he'd been allowed on Stam. By waiting till the very last minute for Dwight's purchase, he could push it on to the next year's accounts. But most interesting of all was that Brian Kidd, then his deputy, didn't rate Dwight, thinking he wasn't much good at beating his man. He wanted to buy John Hartson. Which doesn't say much about Kidd's judgement. But Fergie eventually got his way, and got his man.

 I never thought about the details of the contract, or the money, or anything like that. I just did what Tony said.

After I'd said goodbye to everyone, I got my boots and my medical notes from Jim Walker, the physio, as Tony had told me.

On the way to Manchester in his car, I did ring my mother in Tobago. It was the early hours of the morning there, but she was up. I told her I was joining Manchester United and she said very nice, if that's what you want to do, dear. Oh, I think she knew about Manchester United. She was just being laid back, in Caribbean style.

We stopped before we got to Manchester at some roadside hotel. I went into the toilet and changed from my tracksuit into my suit.

As we got near, Tony briefed me on what to do, about the lay-out of Old Trafford, how to get out of the car quickly and where to head. We knew there would be some press waiting. He told me the main door opened automatically, then I had to go through a sliding door into reception. He'd join me there, after he'd parked the car.

I was then taken away for a medical – to a hospital, don't know which one. They did tests on me. Oh just little tests. Flexing my keee, that sort of thing. I was in a daze really. I hadn't a clue what was happening.

When I came back to Old Trafford, Tony was still in the middle of the contract. I didn't take in anything.

I knew I was not going for the money. Villa had already offered me another contract, with a lot more money, when all this had begun. I knew that, but I wasn't interested in the money. So the details of the contract didn't matter. When Tony said sign here, I just signed.

There was then some legal stuff I had to sign as well, a release form. They said they wouldn't hand over my registration, unless I signed this thing. Something like that. I didn't really understand it. I just signed it, when Tony said it was OK to sign.

I didn't get a penny out of the transfer fee. You don't, these days. The club gets it all.

There was a press conference straight afterwards. I'd never seen so many press people in one room. It was incredible. It let me see just how big Manchester United is. It wasn't as if I was a big inter-national superstar. I'd only come from down the road, from Villa. It was amazing.

They threw lots of questions at me. I made it clear I had not come for the money. The huge transfer, well that was nothing to do with me.

They asked me why I thought I might survive at Manchester United, when other strikers had come and not made it. I just said I was confident in my own ability. I thought I would survive ...

Part 3

MANCHESTER

Manchester United was not always Manchester United. It didn't get that name till 1902, after its predecessor, Newton Heath, went bankrupt. Newton Heath was the waggon works of the Lancashire and Yorkshire Railway Company and some of its workers had got together in 1878 to form a cricket and football club. Typical of the times, from where so many of our major clubs have sprung.

Manchester United was also not always Manchester United. Not in the sense of its modern image as our best-known, most powerful, richest and most followed club. It languished in the old Division Two for long spells in the 1920s and 1930s. Even as recently as 1974–75, it had a season in the Second Division, despite having won the European Cup in 1968, the first English club to do so. (Though Celtic had done it in 1967.)

It was under Sir Matt Busby that they won the European Cup, with George Best and Bobby Charlton. Denis Law, the third of their legendary players, did not play in that game. It was also during Busby's reign that the Munich air disaster had happened, in 1958, when so many of his Busby Babes lost their lives.

Busby retired as manager in 1969, having been in charge

for 24 years. After which, they won the FA Cup several times, but the League Championship eluded them. A long sequence of managers failed to equal the success or achieve the status of Busby, including Mao Tse-tung, or Tommy Docherty as he was then called. Then came the arrival of Alex Ferguson from Aberdeen in 1986.

Like those three other Scots, Jock Stein, Matt Busby and Bill Shankly, Ferguson's early years had been hard and humble. He was born on New Year's Eve 1941, to a family of shipyard workers at Govan, near Glasgow, on the Clyde. He served his apprenticeship as a toolmaker and was involved in a workers' strike. Since then, he has always had an interest and affection for the Labour Party. Oldish Labour rather than Newish Labour.

His own football career, as a battering and battling centre forward, was not particularly distinguished, though he did eventually play for Rangers, his boyhood team. He started in management at East Stirling and St Mirren then went to Aberdeen in 1978 where he completely revitalised the club, breaking the stranglehold on Scottish football traditionally held by Rangers and Celtic, at least for a short while. Under Ferguson, Aberdeen won the Scottish League three times and most impressive of all, beat Real Madrid to win the European Cup Winners' Cup in 1983.

His first two seasons at Manchester United – his first experience of England, as either a player or manager – showed few signs of what was to come. In the 1989–90 season they got hammered by Manchester City 5–1, their traditional rivals. It was assumed by many that if they then got knocked out of the upcoming fourth round of the FA Cup by Notts Forest, that was it, Fergie was on his way out. The fans were critical, the board worried. Fergie himself remembers that period as 'really dark days', skulking round Old Trafford 'like a criminal,' as if he didn't belong there. But they won that cup tie, and went on to the win the 1990 FA Cup – his first big success.

In 1993, Manchester United won the League, now called the Premier League, after an agonising wait of twenty-six years. 'The absence of the Championship,' so Fergie has written, 'had been like a millstone round the neck of everyone connected to the club.' After that, winning trophies became normal, league championships commonplace. Four Premier titles were won in five seasons between 1992 and 1997.

Ferguson's arrival at Manchester United in 1986 coincided with one of the most dramatic periods in English football, the likes of which we have never seen, would never have believed possible in the past and even now, no one can imagine how it will all end. In tears, that's the normal prediction. A revolution fuelled and motivated and run on money is bound to end in bankruptcy for some, so wise heads predict. But not for Manchester United, so even wiser heads assume, not when they are already so rich, already so far ahead.

It was partly created by Sky television, pouring millions into football for television rights, and by the concurrent spawning of vast sponsorship and merchandising deals, along with the arrival of foreign players, made easier by the Bosman rule which allows freedom of movement for players out of contract. So one day we all woke up and found that millionaire footballers had been born.

While Fergie was creating a winning formula on the pitch, off the pitch Manchester United took advantage of all these dramatic changes and rose to become the richest club in Britain. In the whole world, according to a 1999 report in the football magazine, *Four Four Two*.

When he arrived, the permanent staff at Manchester United numbered 140. Today it is around 800. Manchester United's annual income from all sources is now almost

£100 million. Most of this income comes not through the turnstiles, as in ye olden days, which we all thought nature and economics intended, but through merchandising, sponsorship, television and other deals. The value of the club, judged by the bid made for it by Rupert Murdoch's empire in 1998 was £623 million. Most experts today believe its true value is around one billion. You could probably buy Tobago for that.

It's easy to forget how recent all this merchandising mania is. In 1972, when I did a book about Tottenham Hotspur, there were no adverts in their match programmes and no advertising inside the ground. Too vulgar, they thought, too nasty. Arsenal felt the same. They did not need to stoop so low. As for the idea of a commercial sponsor's name on the front of an Arsenal or Spurs shirt, the very idea was considered obscene.

Even when Fergie arrived at Manchester United, such notions were still considered vulgarities in most leading clubs. Manchester United had no shirt sponsor until the early 1980s and no club shop selling repro shirts till the latter part of the decade. Now merchandising brings in around £25 million a year. Their Megastore serves 6,000 customers every home game who can buy everything from pens to bedspreads in Manchester United colours. Well, not quite everything. They have turned down Manchester United coffins and Manchester United condoms and even said no to Manchester United toilet paper. That would doubtless have sold well – among Manchester City supporters. In 1998, they opened a new £4million museum which attracts 200,000 visitors a season. A whole chain of Manchester United shops, selling only Manchester United goods, is now being planned to be opened worldwide.

In England, it is estimated there are four million Manchester United fans – 98 per cent of whom will never see the team play. Even with the biggest club stadium in

England, currently holding 55,000, but soon to be expanded yet again to hold 67,400 by 2001, they can never accommodate all those who want to come.

Strange in a way that Manchester United's modern merchandising mania and the arrival of millionaire players should have happened under Fergie, someone from a totally different generation, who played his football at a time when even star players still travelled on the bus to training and lived a life similar to other skilled members of the working classes. In his 1997 diary *A Will to Win*, he is considering buying Karel Poborsky but worries that 'his hair may well get on my nerves if I sign him'.

Hard to imagine such a thought occurring to, say, Terry Venables, a much flasher, more modern figure, who has worked abroad, unlike Fergie, always interested in money matters – if not always successfully.

A player's long hair, or more likely his shaven head, is the least of worries for today's manager, not when there are so many other distractions for his millionaire players, such as drugs, booze, fast cars, fast women, fast lifestyles, dodgy agents and interfering sponsors.

Busby never managed to keep Best in check, yet Fergie has proved tougher, more dictatorial, more protective with his young charges. Very few have let him down or shown his judgement to be faulty. He is known to be a screamer and shouter in the dressing room.

In his 1997 diary, he tells how he was at a football function in Morecambe when someone mentioned in passing that Ryan Giggs and Lee Sharpe had been seen having a night out in Blackpool the previous Monday, just two days before a vital match. Fergie was so furious at hearing this that he left the function at once, drove back to Manchester, went straight to Lee Sharpe's house in order to reprimand him – and discovered, by chance, there was a party going on.

'The place was bursting with music and girls. They even

had the apprentices there. It didn't go on much longer, not after I'd kicked a few doors and a few backsides ...'

This incident took place in 1992. Since then, he is said to have mellowed somewhat. So today's players hope.

In his own private life, he has been happily married to Cathy for over 30 years. They have three sons, two of them twins, and three grandchildren, who include twin girls. Like most managers, modern or traditional, his family life has often taken second place to football. He forgot his wife's Christmas present once, giving her a cheque instead. She immediately tore it up. Sounds a spirited woman. On his return from some foreign defeat, she was waiting at the front door for him, chanting 'Fergie, Fergie, for the sack.'

Not much chance of that, not any more. It's safe to assume that Fergie will go when Fergie decides to go. Manchester United is today not just a rich club but also a stable club with a long-reigning manager. Unlike Villa. In Dwight's nine seasons there, he had served under five different managers.

So Dwight, when he arrived at the beginning of the 1998–99 season, was achieving his heart's desire, to play for the nation's top, most secure club, with the best manager, joining arguably the best set of players.

And yet, at that moment when he arrived, they were fail-ures. By their new and extremely high standards. A whole season had gone by without one pot. Arsenal had pipped them to the 1998 Premier title and they had been knocked out of the European Championship in the quarter finals. In his introduction to the official book about Manchester United's 1997–98 season, Fergie had described his disap-pointment. 'It was a bitter pill to swallow. I have never felt so low in football.'

All comparative of course. Surely there had been some far more skunnering moments at St Mirren. But that's life, when you reach the top. The stakes are higher, the pressures greater. Hence his determination to improve the squad for the season ahead, signing Jaap Stam on 1 July 1998 for £10.75 million, Jesper Blomqvist for £4.4 million on 21 July 1998 and finally Dwight in August – a total of £28 million in a month.

A fortunate time to arrive? Yes, in the sense that it's always best to come in when things are down. You can then take some of the credit if things go up. But players in forward positions, such as Dwight, had not been all that fortunate at Manchester United in recent years, failing to adapt, be accepted by the fans, do the business. Poborksy had gone back to Europe, without leaving much of a mark.

More worrying was the example of Teddy Sheringham who, like Dwight, had arrived from another English club, where he had been highly successful. He had joined exactly one year earlier from Spurs. Fergie had seen him as partly a replacement for Cantona, which was a burden for a start. Cantona had dominated Manchester United by his play and his personality.

Sheringham had started inauspiciously, missing a penalty at Spurs, then was dropped after Manchester United got beaten by Barnsley in the FA Cup. But it got worse, as he bravely admitted in his biography. (*Teddy Sheringham*, published by Little, Brown, 1998).

'The crowd lashed into me towards the end of the season. I don't think they ever really appreciated what I was doing for the team. The key to discovering whether you're doing things more or less right is the other players' response to you. I always say the definition of a good player is someone the others want in their team. In a season in which I played OK sometimes, and not so well on other occasions, I don't think I had the full respect of the other players. You feel it. You don't have to be told ...'

Poor Teddy. Yet he had arrived as a mature, experienced, intelligent player aged 30. Dwight was younger with no family support and with little of Teddy's foreign or international experience. Would he cope at Manchester United or would he crumble?

29 After I'd signed and done the press conference, I stayed in Manchester – I didn't go back to my house in Birmingham. Not for weeks. And that was just to pick up some clothes.

I stayed the first night at the Copthorne Hotel then I went to Mottram Park, the hotel Manchester United uses. I think I was there a week. Then I moved to the Alderley Edge Hotel. Altogether, I lived in a hotel for four months. Yeah, it was a long time.

I don't really like living in a hotel. It's true that as a single person it shouldn't really matter. It wasn't that I was being separated from a wife or family or partner. But in a hotel, you don't get any privacy. People know who is coming to your room, what you are eating and drinking, who you are ringing. And when you join a club like Manchester United, you don't have much privacy any more. That was about the first big lesson I had to learn.

I thought arriving at Villa was an enormous change for me, with their setup and facilities, compared with Tobago, but Manchester United was different again – not just in size and scale but also in the attention you get. You can't escape from it. Everything you do, everywhere you go, you are spotted. There are people looking out for you, and not necessarily to do you any favours.

On the football side, the first few days were difficult. I arrived with no friends at the club, though I had met Coley and Giggs at various places. And I had met Becks through Tony [Stephens, his agent]. But I didn't have what you'd call a friend there, not like the ones I'd left behind at Villa.

Yeah, I did wonder how I would fit in. Manchester United is a

Big Club full of Big Names. No disrespect to Villa, but I knew it would be much harder to fit in and do well.

I signed on the Thursday evening and on the Friday morning I was taken to the Cliff [Manchester United's training ground]. Otherwise I would never have found it. The kit man, Albert Morgan, took me into the dressing room and told me where to sit.

I went round and shook hands with everyone. No one really introduced me, said this is Dwight. I just went round the room and said hello to everyone.

It was only a light training session that first day, just half an hour, as we were going to travel that afternoon to London, for the match against West Ham.

Although it was just a light session, I could sense that Keano [Roy Keane, the captain] was testing me. From about five yards away, he belted this awkward ball at me, as if to say 'deal with this'.

I did, bringing it under control. I smiled and said, 'Cheers, mate.' I'm not sure if he did it deliberately, but that's how I saw it. But that was all. There were no tricks, no jokes played on me, no remarks, not in the first few days anyway.

After a few weeks, when I'd got used to training with them, then the obvious remarks came out. Oh you know, the obvious things. If I missed a shot, or put a header wide in those early weeks, someone would say 'Twelve and a half million, bloody hell'. You have to get used to that. We all do it.

I didn't expect to play in that West Ham game, as I had literally just arrived. I hadn't even trained with them properly. I thought I'd be on the bench, but the Gaffer said to me, no, you're playing.

He had told me that he just wanted me to be myself. 'You know who you're playing for now,' he said. 'If you can't play here, you can't play anywhere.' Before the match he just told me to enjoy myself.

I was so psyched up, so wanting to do well, that, well, it didn't really happen. I wanted to play my normal game, and not worry about it too much, but I couldn't help it. It was a 0–0 draw. I played average, let's say. So, yeah, I was disappointed.

It was lucky for me in a way that Becks was the centre of attention, not me. It was not long after the World Cup and his sending off and there was supposed to be a big demonstration against him, with red cards all round the ground, so we were led to believe.

There was a lot of booing, every time he got the ball, but he dealt with it brilliantly. I don't know how he did it, how he coped. Anyway, it took the attention away from me.

On Monday, on the way to training at the Cliff, I got completely lost. It was the first time I'd gone on my own. I had to ring Coley on my mobile. He directed me while driving his car, told me which motorway to get on and off. I was miles away from it, going the wrong way. But luckily I'd set off in lots of time, so I wasn't really late.

My home debut was on the following Saturday – against Charlton. That was more important than the West Ham match, playing at home for the first time.

Luckily for me, it went well. I got two goals and we won 4–0. Ole [Gunnar Solskjaer] got the others. From then on, I never felt any worries. I felt accepted and part of the club. I felt at home.

Gary Neville is the solid, serious one in the Manchester United dressing room. Scholes, Butt and Cole are also fairly serious, but quiet with it, not drawing attention to themselves. Gary is prefect material, first to arrive for training, willing to be seen as a goody goody, even if the rest of the team takes the mickey out of him. Born nearby in Bury, he joined Manchester United as a trainee aged 16 in 1991 – and before that he used to stand on the terraces, supporting Manchester United. He and his younger brother Phil signed seven-and-a-half-year contracts in 1998, the longest ever signed at Manchester United.

He has been best friends with Beckham since they signed as trainees on the same day, 8 July 1991, though they could hardly be more different. Gary is dour, canny, northern. Becks is glamorous, showy, southern. Stereotypical descriptions, but roughly pretty true.

Gary, for example, does not believe in agents. 'It would upset me if ever I had to give a penny to an agent on my club or boot contracts.' His father Neville Neville, an ex-player, who now works for Bury, deals with any business enquiries. Yes, Neville Neville. Roy Keane's joke is that their grandad is called Neville Neville Neville.

Becks has often tried to get Gary to splash out, live a bit, spend a bit. While shopping with Gary in Manchester, Becks once tried to persuade him to buy an £8,500 Rolex watch. 'No chance. Anyway I've never worn a watch in my life.'

Gary used to share a bedroom with Becks, when playing abroad for England. To his astonishment, after a match in Georgia, Gary was sent a phone bill for £800. It turned out to be half of a £1600 phone bill for their room which Becks had run up in two days, ringing his girlfriend. Gary asked for a room of his own from then on.

He gets teased for being so northern, so solid and sensible, just as Becks gets teased for being Becks, and for having a funny southern accent. Ryan Giggs says that he never knew what Becks was saying in training when he shouted, ''It it'. And they are all amused when Becks is showing off his latest flash, luxury motor and warns them before getting in 'don't scuff me levver'.

Roy Keane is the main joker, the main winder-up of people liable to be wound up. Gary is often the butt of such jokes, which he can take of course, being ever sensible, then he'll tell them against himself.

When the rest of the team heard that Gary was going to be best man at Beckham's wedding, Roy Keane offered to take bets on how quickly everyone would fall asleep during his speech. As for the stag night, which Gary would have to organise, they all guessed it would be held at the snooker club in Bury. Hee hee.

All dressing rooms have their own codes, their own language and legends. There is always a moaner, a joker, a tight one, a flash one, one who rushes off, one who stays, one who is quiet, gets picked upon, one who is noisy and loud. Any dressing room is hard for a complete outsider to enter, until you know the grammar, pick up the ways.

At Manchester United, a dressing room full of stars, a newcomer might think he knows most of them already, by their fame and reputation, but players are not always as depicted in the tabloids, or as they might appear on the park. David May, for example. Quiet, nervous, hesitant perhaps off the pitch? Nope. In the dressing room, he is just as noisy as Roy Keane, practical joking, mocking others.

Another possible difficulty, for absolute beginners, is the fact that Manchester United, despite being able to spend millions on foreign stars, has a hard core of players who have been at Manchester United since they were in nappies, like Becks and the Nevilles, Butt and Scholes. Their friendships are long-formed, their knowledge of how Manchester United works, who really matters, is long-forged.

So, Gary, what did yous all think about Yorkie, when he first walked into your dressing room?

'Well, like most transfers at Manchester United, there was a build up beforehand. You hear rumours, read things – then mostly it never happens.

'With Dwight, there had been stories running for about three months. You try to take no notice. I didn't really, till one morning the manager walks in with Dwight – and that was the first we knew about it.'

With Fergie? Dwight thought he himself went round saying hello, and was not formally introduced. Perhaps half introduced, then, half taken round.

'On his first day at training, I'm sure he was probably a

bit nervous, but he didn't show it. He just wore a huge smile all the time.

'I can remember playing against him, when he was still at Villa. It was the first match of the '95 season and I was playing at centre back. They beat us 3–1. I remember then being impressed by Dwight. He struck me as a complete forward. He wasn't all that prolific a scorer at that time, but he had so many extra qualities – holding the ball, bringing people into play, as well as scoring. I couldn't see any weaknesses.

'His first match for us, against West Ham, was a dull affair. I have to admit we didn't get much service up to Andy and Dwight. On that day's showing, it was hard to predict how well they would play together – or even if they would be considered as the main partnerships.

'Dwight was lucky of course scoring in his first home match. That's so vital for a striker. Until you start scoring, you don't quite have the crowd on your side, that's if you're a striker. It irradicated any problems he might have had – even before they started.'

Dwight scored again in the next match, against Coventry City. Again a home match and, like the three previous games, Andy Cole had been left on the bench – suggesting that in Fergie's mind, his front pairing could be Dwight and Solskjaer, with Cole and Sheringham as subs. This was the same in the next game, the home leg of the European Championship tie against Barcelona which finished 3–3.

In the next league game, they were stuffed 3–0 by Arsenal. Ryan Giggs partnered Dwight up front, with Blomqvist on the left wing, which clearly didn't work.

Dwight scored again in their next European match, against Bayern Munich, which was another draw, 2–2. Dwight was paired this time with Sheringham, with Andy Cole still on the bench.

It wasn't till 3 October, that Dwight and Andy began up front together, the first time since Dwight's debut game. It was a 3–0 victory, with Dwight and Cole each scoring. The following week, they demolished Wimbledon 5–1, with Andy getting two and Dwight one. The week after, they beat Brondby 6–2. Cole and Dwight got one each.

So, after several permutations, some false and misleading combinations, the partnership up front between Dwight and Cole looked by far the best. Dwight was scoring regularly, but also helping Cole to score, laying on chances for him, almost as if it had always been the obvious, natural partnership. It hadn't. Dwight and Cole do look vaguely similar, in height, build, speed, each 5ft 10in and 12st 4lb. Conventional wisdom suggests that if you have two forwards, they should offer contrasts, different sorts of threats to the opposition, even if the contrast is simplistic like one big and one small. A big bloke in the air, who knocks it down for the other such as say Toshack and Keegan. Or a quick one and a slower one. A quick one who can dart in, be a goal poacher, a finisher like Jimmy Greaves, who doesn't do much else, while the slower one, the grafter, sets up the chances.

What happened with Cole and Dwight was that while having similar qualities and skills, they seemed to understand and anticipate what the other would do, would want to do, despite never having played together before. They didn't duplicate but doubled, if not tripled, their possibilities and threats. The passing between them, their anticipation and speed, often gave the opposition the impression there might be three of them floating and flying through their defence.

Dwight, as the newcomer, was given most praise for creating this surprising partnership, making it work, giving Cole the sort of chances and confidence he had not always had before, but it was a mutual thing, which they did together.

Alex Ferguson had always worried about Cole's confidence. 'Players like Andy can sometimes pick up one small piece of criticism and magnify it,' so Ferguson wrote in his diary, *A Will to Win*. 'The key is definitely his confidence.'

But now with Dwight beside him, all that seemed to have

changed, as Fergie admitted. 'It was a piece of luck. My job was to get Yorke into this club. What I'd wanted, what I'd planned, was for him to play alongside Kluivert because I felt we needed a physical presence back in the club. We'd been a bit lightweight.'

Patrick Kluivert, of course, didn't come, but you can see the thinking, wondering that Dwight and Andy might not have enough presence when playing together. 'But when Yorkie and Andy clicked, wow! What I think Yorkie has done for Cole is he's made him more relaxed. He looked at how Yorkie was, how relaxed, and he's thought, this is possible. And he's taken a bit of that manner on. I mean, Yorkie, what a personality. He misses a sitter – and he smiles.'

So fortunate for Fergie, and Andy Cole and the rest of the team, 'We're lucky at Manchester United in having four quality strikers,' says Gary Neville. 'Each one was tried with Dwight in turn – which is a compliment to Dwight. He managed so well with each one, changed his game to fit in with them. But of course it was when his partnership with Andy gelled, that it really worked, when we really started buzzing.

'I think in the second game against Barcelona, the 3–3 draw, they showed the best forward play I have ever witnessed. Honestly. Either as a player or spectator. The two of them together ran Barcelona ragged. They were unbelievable. Out of this world.'

31 *One surprise to me, when I first arrived at Manchester United, was that we do less training than we did at Villa. Less work, I mean.*
The Gaffer won't let you do anything extra.
At Villa, I and several others always did lots of extra work, staying on after anyone else, doing extra things. The Gaffer won't allow it.

Even at the very beginning of the season, he restricted it. It was as if he knew we were going to be in so many finals, and have so many pressure matches, so he wanted us to pace ourselves properly during the season.

As for the actual training, well that's basically much the same as we did at Villa. The only real difference is that we have so many quality players. You notice it all the time.

I did try to do some extra training early on. The Gaffer came on the pitch, hugged me – and carted me off. That's when the lads started asking if he was my Dad. That's still one of the dressing-room jokes. 'Did the Gaffer bring you breakfast in bed then?' That's the sort of stuff they'll ask.

I'm told from the other players that he wasn't so relaxed in the old days. People were scared of him then. He could really let fly. He does often go barmy at half times in the dressing room, but then he carries on afterwards, as if nothing happened, playing cards with you or whatever.

He knows what each of us is capable of, so if he takes a pop at you, the chances are you deserve it. I've had a couple of bollockings, but that's about all.

At first I used to think the dressing-room atmosphere was very quiet. Before a match, I mean. At least it seemed quieter than at Villa. But once I settled in, I livened things up. Oh yeah.

I like to mess around with a ball in the dressing room, just to liven things up. Me and Butty play two-touch headers, in the dressing room, or I play at volleying the ball into his hands. It does ping around the dressing room, but no, no one complains. I don't think at Manchester United we have people who want absolute silence before a match. Well, I don't anyway.

I wasn't noisy at first of course. You have to crawl before you can walk. You watch and observe what others do, before you can then just be yourself.

I think the crowd took to me from the beginning. Some of them sang the song about me they sang at Villa, to the tune of 'New York, New York', but perhaps not quite as loud.

Then they started a rude song about me. Oh you know why.

Because of all the press stories and other rubbish. I'm not repeating the words. I wouldn't like children to hear it. It doesn't bother me. It just makes me smile. Mostly though I can't really hear what they're singing.

When all those kiss-and-tell stories first started in the papers, I went to see the Gaffer. No, I don't feel closer to him than anyone else does, but I wanted to confide in him, tell him the whole truth, confess what I'd done and not done. I want him on my side, don't I? I want him to know the truth.

His attitude is that unless it affects your football, then it's OK with him. That's how it should be ...

 That was one thing Dwight did not quite expect, when he moved to Manchester. As a single man, he had had lots of girlfriends, ever since he was a young teenager in Tobago, when the girls first started going after him. Nothing ever really made the papers, as he was just another single footballer, enjoying himself the way single footballers do. And married footballers, but we won't go into all that.

With a club like Manchester United, which has a national, if not international name, any personal titbits are likely to make the newspapers. And if they are personal titbits of a sexual nature, well, they can command quite a price.

There are females who go out of their way to sleep with famous footballers, like groupies who follow pop stars around, not necessarily to write about it afterwards, just to notch up points. They can be quite troublesome, if repelled, cause scenes in clubs or pubs. There are also males in pubs who want a share, to rub shoulders, shake hands with the stars, who see them as familiars, part of their own lives, who feel they are real friends, and if not personal friends, then public property. If repelled, they too can get nasty, pick fights, invite the star to step aside, and see how hard he is. Oh it can be tough these days, being a star player. One has to feel a certain sympathy.

For the normal film star, pop star, tycoon, politician, part of their fantasising from when they are little is to have all the sex they can get, when they have made it. It keeps them going, during the years of struggle. Football stars, being simpler souls, see themselves at Wembley, passing to Hoddle, or whoever their boyhood hero was, then driving away in a flash car. Extra sex is a by-product of their fame, rarely a guiding star.

The sex stories about Dwight started the moment he arrived at Manchester. On 29 August, before he had hardly found his peg in the Manchester United dressing room, the *Sun* cleared its whole front page to announce: 'VIDEO SHAME OF £12m YORKE'. What must the good, God-fearing teachers and people of Bon Accord have thought of that. Not to mention Shustoke.

After that came regular coverage, eight similar stories over the next eight months, in both the Sunday and daily tabloids, with girls telling about their nights of passion with him, his feats of sexual athleticism, often carefully concealing the fact that these relationships, most of them fleeting, had happened some time ago. One girl did describe him as 'gentle, loving and affectionate in bed'. Which was kind. While another claimed he had told her he was a postman. Which was very confusing.

In Shustoke, Mums got very upset. 'Of course he has girlfriends,' says Sheila. 'He's a single man, but if you believe all the stuff in the papers, you'll believe anything.

'That story about the video comes from a Vicars and Tarts party – the women dressed as men, the men as women. It took place in Birmingham, not Manchester, and was a harmless party, not an orgy. Someone took a video of it, as you do at any family party. The paper is supposed to have found the video in a dustbin – but I don't believe it. Someone sold it to them, if you ask me. They then made it look like an orgy, but nothing happened.'

I asked how Sheila was so sure. She said she knew the housekeeper of the player's house in question, and when cleaning up she found no evidence of any orgy. So there. She then gave me a blow-by-blow account of another saga, one where she had personally been present, as a guest of Dwight's.

'It was during the weekend away at a charity match. This girl arrived wearing what looked like a night dress, no bra, all dolled up. We went to the match together. I asked if she'd ever been to a match before and she hadn't. She was soon freezing in her silly clothes. I was jumping up and down all the time when Dwight touched the ball.

'"I can't believe a woman of your age can get so excited," she says to me.

'I had a drink with her later and I said to her, "Can you cook?" She said, "No." "If you get involved with Dwight, who's going to do the cooking then?" "Oh," she says, "we'll eat out all the time." "Dwight won't like that," I says. "He likes his roast beef and Yorkshire pudding at home, does Dwight." She was one of them model types. They can't do anything.

'During that weekend, she can hardly have been with Dwight for more than an hour or so, yet she goes and sells all that stuff to the paper.

'It happens all the time. One girl demanded £4,000 from Dwight for a boob job. When he refused, she sold her story for £5,000. Some of them have got as much as £50,000. So I'm told. Almost all of it is lies.

'I've warned him that if he does let one of them move into his new house with him, they could claim half of his estate. That's the law now, oh yes. I also worry that one of them will just disappear with all his belongings.

'You can't blame the girls for going after him – he is so lovable. If some girl comes to his house with her knickers in her handbag, it's up to him, isn't it? As my mother always used to say, "If there were no bad women, there would be no bad men".

'Who wouldn't love him? He's adorable. And he's never ever horrible to anyone. You won't hear him slagging people off or criticising. Even when Milosevic [Savo, ex Villa striker] was keeping him out of the team, and he had a bad game, I would say "that Milosovic, he's bloody useless." Dwight would say "No, he'll come good." You'll never hear a bad word from him.

'I know he didn't get on with John Gregory in the end, but he won't say anything against him. Mention the name Gregory, and he'll change the subject.'

Very true, Sheila. I was having that problem myself. Not that I was wanting Dwight to rubbish other people, well not really, but he does choose his words very carefully, unwilling to give offence which often means in the process he gives very little away.

Sheila was and is in regular touch with Dwight, despite his move to Manchester.

'He rings twice a week. The other week he rang me after one of those terrible Sunday paper scandal stories. I was just so upset by it. People I met locally kept on saying to me "was it true, not your Dwight, ohhh". It was terrible, for him and of course poor Grace, his mother.

'Then do you know what he did? He said to me, "To make up for all you've been through on my behalf, here's the tickets for a holiday." He sent me and Bryn to Minorca. Two weeks, all paid. Wasn't that marvellous? Typical of him. So generous and kind.

'I've been to Manchester to see him play a few times and he always gets us tickets for the players lounge afterwards.'

Sheila has been going to Villa for some 15 years, as a

surrogate mum to scores of young players, invited into their inner sanctums. I imagined she probably didn't enjoy Old Trafford as much, perhaps finding it intimidating after the homeliness of Villa.

'Oh no,' she said. 'We much prefer Manchester United. The first time I was in the players' lounge, Nicky Butt's mother came up and looked after me. Wasn't that nice? All the mothers were so kind. Fetching me drinks and that. In Villa's players' lounge, you don't get drinks anymore, just tea and sandwiches. Oh no. John Gregory has banned alcohol. That hasn't happened yet at Old Trafford. Fortunately.

'It's all much more organised at Manchester United as well. I've been on at them at Villa for years to get me car parking, especially since Bryn became disabled. All the years I've worked for them, yet you have to pay for almost every little thing.

'Now at Manchester United, you park in this place, a bit away, but it's special parking, then a security man picks you up and drives you to the front door. Then you get escorted to your seat. Isn't that good? And the food and drink are terrific. Sausage rolls, chicken drumsticks, things on sticks, anything you want to eat or drink. Oh it's marvellous, at Manchester United.'

Certainly is. No wonder it's the ambition of every healthy normal boy to play there. Despite the drawbacks of mega fame and constant media attention.

The sex stories in the papers have been the worst thing that's happened to me, ever, in my career. It was horrible. I got really depressed. I just didn't expect it would be as bad.

I now know it comes with the territory. When you join Manchester United, your profile becomes huge. People come out of the woodwork and sell any old story about you. When girls allege something has happened to them, in a club or wherever, they don't ring the police – they ring the newspapers, straight away, and demand money.

Yeah, the Andy Cole story, me and Andy with a girl story. That really was the worst.

I think people do these things in order to wreck relationships – and of course to make money. But that was the worst ever. I mean I'm single, but Andy has a long-time partner and a child. I like his girlfriend, always got on well with her, and their little boy. But when that story happened, well, it looked all my fault, didn't it, as if I'd led him astray.

If it had been just about me, I would have shrugged it off, not been bothered too much. I've done nothing illegal, done nothing wrong. I go out, I meet girls, I'm not denying it. I do do certain things. But this time, with Andy dragged into it, it was horrible.

I went to see his girlfriend. I tried to explain it to her. It was pretty true about me, but not about Andy. What they said about Andy never happened. I told her that.

I did feel for Andy, that it was in the papers. I was very low. Yeah, the worst thing I've gone through in my career.

After that, our relationship for a time was a bit strained. We are still friends, but it slackened off a bit. It wasn't quite what it was. But now we're fine, on and off the pitch. These stories happen. They just exaggerate it.

I could sue, but what good would that do? They'd just print a little correction, if they print anything at all. But I can handle it. It's when others are dragged into it.

It didn't happen at Villa. And I did the same sort of things. Here at Manchester United, it's different. You're the hottest, playing for Manchester United, so people come after you, looking to cause trouble. One thing about the Gaffer is that he understands what these people are like. He supports you. That's the beauty of the Gaffer.

I suppose I am marked now. I am a target for these stories, so people will believe any of them. The strange thing is that at all clubs there are people, married people and single people, who do much the same thing – but they get away with it. Nobody knows. They don't get in the papers. I have had to take the blame in the past, cover up for people.

It has made me more wary. Not cynical. That's not in my nature. I'm still polite when strangers come up to me to ask for an autograph or whatever. But in public I am more reserved than I was. I have become more aware of things and people around me.

The other thing about Manchester United, so everyone told me before I came, would be the hatred, that so many people hate them. At Villa, I didn't like them, because they were always successful. It wasn't real hatred. Just rivalry.

But I realise now, wherever we go, there will be people really hating us, out of jealousy of course.

No, I haven't heard any Munich songs. What sort? No, I haven't heard anything. But then I don't really listen to the songs from the opposition fans.

I just want to concentrate on playing football. And it's been brilliant. The season's gone really well.

I suppose the best game, so far, the one which gave me the best feeling, was against Liverpool in the FA Cup [24 January 1999]. We beat them and I scored. Ole got a goal as well. I thought that was my best game.

My best goal of the season, to me, was against West Ham, at Old Trafford. Shaka Hislop, my old buddy, was in goal for them. Beforehand I had a bet on with him. If I scored a goal against him, he'd buy me a drink. If I didn't score, I'd buy the drinks.

I did score, from a very acute angle. So that was good. And I did get the drink out of him afterwards.

Overall, it's been great. I expected it to be good, but not this good. It's ten times better than I ever expected.

I've felt no pressure all season. When I arrived, the Gaffer never said I had to score so many goals. I think if he had, I might not have signed. That's the sort of pressure no one wants. He's not put any pressure on me. He's been very relaxed with me.

The pressures come from the media, and their stories. I just want to be left alone to play football.

After that, all I want to do is sit at home, or in a hotel room with my buddies, play cards and have a few drinks. I don't want all that hassle ...

34 On my first visit to see Dwight in his new £600,000 home, I sent the taxi away, thinking I'm here, this is clearly the right house, no problem. He'd moved in only a month or so earlier, in Bramhall, deep in stockbroker Cheshire. The house from outside looked brand new, brick built, long and low, Beverly Hills posh.

Through the gate, down the driveway, I could see three cars, so I presumed he must be back from training. He has a £150,000 Ferrari, commonplace among today's young men playing for Manchester United. Beckham, Giggs, Cole, Butt and Sheringham were all running around in a Ferrari. Dwight's is a 550 Maranello, whatever that means. Could it be connected with that languid Scot who once played for Arsenal? He also has a Mercedes, top of the range by the look of it, and a Range Rover.

I walked up to the intercom on the high security gates and pressed, waiting to hear a voice answering. Nothing happened. I pressed again, then realised to my horror it was the sort of high security intercom where you need a secret code before they even answer the intercom. Why the hell had I sent the taxi away, before I was actually in the house?

Looking up and down the tree-lined avenue, I could see no signs of human life. As I waited, the heavens opened. I was in my white suit, well off-white, my only vaguely

Dwight Yorke signs for Manchester United in August 1998. (Above) With manager Alex Ferguson. (Below) With Ferguson and chairman Martin Edwards.
JOHN PETERS

(Above) Dwight Yorke thunders through the Liverpool defence during the FA Cup fourth-round match on 24 January 1999. COLORSPORT

(Left) Dwight, Manchester United's top scorer in 1998/9. EMPICS

(Right) Dwight Yorke celebrates with David Beckham and the FA Cup after the 1999 final victory over Newcastle United. ACTION IMAGES

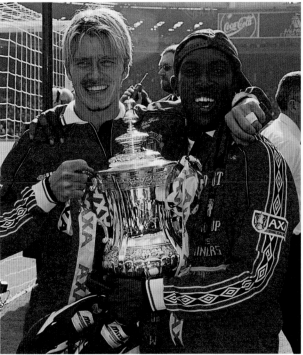

(Above) Yorke and
Cole with team-mate
Gary Neville.
COLORSPORT

(Left) The celebrated
partnership. Dwight
with Andy Cole.
ACTION IMAGES

(Right) Team-mate
Mark Bosnich.
COLORSPORT

(Above) Alex Ferguson presents Dwight Yorke with the club Player of the Year
award on 1 May 1999. EMPICS

(Left) Yorke's captain, Roy Keane. COLORSPORT

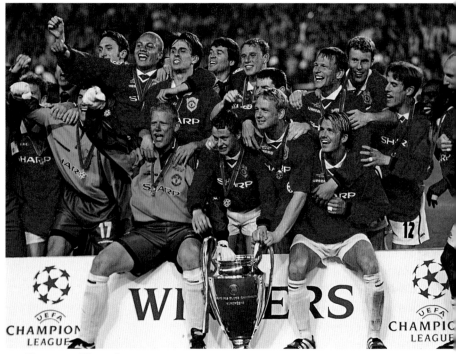

European Champions. ACTION IMAGES

Celebrating the Treble, May 1999. On the triumphal tour of Manchester, Dwight's cigar is his symbol of success. And also of his Tobago roots? (The name Tobago comes from tobacco.) ACTION IMAGES

smartish outfit, just a cheap one, which immediately crumpled and collapsed and looked as if I'd been sleeping on a beach. Appearances matter to footballers, always have done. I had thought of driving here in my Jag, even though it is five years old. It was just as well. It would have looked a bit shoddy, beside all those modern motors.

I walked to a junction and stood near a post box, waiting. A woman with a dog arrived, to post a letter. She had no idea where the nearest public phone box was. And no, she certainly did not have a mobile phone.

I went back to the house, tried another mad combination of numbers and letters on the intercom, jumped up and down, did a bit of shouting. Should I climb over his wall, dash across the manicured lawns and borders, which looked as if they had been laid this morning? The front windows were closed. Perhaps he hadn't returned from training after all. Or had he forgotten our meeting? Having your biography written when you are only 27 might seem quite an event, to a normal person of 27, but not to a super star millionaire footballer in 1999. More like a minor irritation, another draggy thing to go through.

That was the day I decided to buy a mobile phone, something I'd always mocked. I had Dwight's home number, but no way of ringing him. If he was inside, and had heard some idiot shouting, he probably thought it was the *News of the World* or *Sun*, trying to doorstep him. Or another dopey girl, trying to break into his life.

In the end, I walked for half a mile to a stately home, Bramall Hall, where I persuaded a girl in the kitchen to let me use her phone and I rang Dwight, asking him to open his bloody gate.

He was all smiles, which the football world, and Sheila, know and love. Wearing a crew neck jumper with the name Armani in sideways writing, jeans and sandals and bare feet.

He led me through a marble hall, very interior designed, which I naturally admired, as that's the point of having an interior designer. We went into his back kitchen where a television was blaring away. This was where he had been sitting, at the back of the house, so he'd not seen me at the front gate.

There was a girl there and he introduced her politely. I took her to be someone to do with the design or furnishings of the house as he was still having things re-done.

The girl said she would go in another room while we talked and read a book. She went to an arty, wrought-iron bookcase where there were two books – a biography of Brian Lara and one on Kevin Keegan. She took the Kevin Keegan and went off.

Dwight asked if I'd like anything to eat or drink. I said a beer would be nice. He then gave me his full attention, and he did put the television down slightly, which was thoughtful. We talked for three hours on that visit, without a pause, apart from various telephone calls. He seemed to have a battery of mobile and assorted phones. One of his callers was Brian Lara. Another was Mark Bosnich.

When we finished the formal part of our chat, taking him slowly through various bits of his career, he switched the TV up again. It was Sky Sports and Andy Gray was analysing the previous Sunday's Manchester United game with Middlesbrough, in which Dwight had had a goal disallowed for offside. Andy was taking us through it, with clever diagrams, explaining Dwight's movements and body language, what he was trying to do or not do.

It must be strange, I said, listening to yourself being discussed.

'No,' said Dwight flatly.

I mean seeing yourself up there, watching your own movements being analysed, while you sit here.

'No,' he said, just as flatly. 'Why?'

Well, I said, doesn't it seem as if there are two of you, one up there, one here.

'No,' he said.

So that was the end of that line of idle chat. When I was interviewing the Beatles, many years ago, when they were the most famous, most discussed persons on the planet, I had a similar conversation. They indulged me, but I don't think their answers were any more illuminating.

Throughout the serious, biographical part of our chat, Dwight was helpful, thoughtful, interested, without revealing very much about himself, or his real thoughts, his real opinions. But I had got what I had come for, covered the stage in his life I'd wanted him to talk about.

When I left, I remembered the girl and felt rather sorry for her, being stuck with Kevin Keegan for all those hours.

In the cab, which Dwight ordered for me, back to Stockport station, the minicab driver said everyone locally loved Dwight.

I'd gathered that, I said. Everyone says the same. Lovely bloke, always smiling.

'We have a lot of footballers round here, from City and United, and we love them all. Because of the girls. We spend half our lives picking them up. They keep us in business. We'd be lost without them ...'

On my next appointment, a few weeks later, he kept me waiting for two hours. But at least I was able to ring him on my mobile phone. I found out he was still at the Cliff, a longer training session than expected, and some meetings. It was now getting towards the end of the season. Things were hotting up.

I walked to Bramall Hall, sat outside in the sun and had tea and a bun and read Gary and Phil Neville's Manchester United diary, *For Club and Country*. What impressed me about Gary was his sincere attempt to fill in his diary. I could see him sucking his pencil, determined to record his thoughts, however mundane, however routine. Would I ever get Dwight to sit down and give me his thoughts?

He arrived home just before five, in his Ferrari, looking grim, not his usual smiley self. It was clear the last thing he wanted was to sit down and have a serious converstion. When this happened with John Lennon, I'd swim round his pool with him for an hour, not talking, then sit watching TV with him for another hour, still not talking. Then go home. He was often half stoned, so talking was not always an option.

Dwight said he was shattered, hadn't slept much last night, felt exhausted, so I said don't worry, I won't go through the stuff I'd planned to talk about. I'll just hang about for a bit. He got himself something to eat, taking a ready-made meal from the fridge and putting it in the microwave. It was rice and stew. He hoped I didn't mind, he said politely, sitting at a table and eating, but he was starving. Then he switched on TV.

'Watch this,' he said, putting the sound up. 'This is a girl I really like.'

I looked at the screen and there was a man reading the news.

'She's usually on at this time,' he said.

Do you know her?

'Oh yes. I've met her.'

When she was clearly not going to appear, and he had finished eating, I asked if I could have a look round his house, which I hadn't done on the last visit.

He took me round it, half heartedly. Every room on the ground floor seemed the same – white carpets, white walls, expensive pieces of marble, glass, polished wood, all of it unused, unlived in. Seemed mad, all these reception rooms, for one person, living on his own. Had he had a house-warming party yet?

'No, and I won't. You know what will happen. The papers will turn it into an orgy.'

Upstairs, I didn't count the bedrooms, probably four or five, all with white carpets, devoid of any personality. His own bedroom was equally stark. All I could see was a king-size bed with one of his leather jackets thrown over it. This was about the only sign that someone actually lived in the house. Sometimes. He hadn't actually been home for three days.

The only signs of real life were in a corridor, leading off his bedroom, where his clothes were kept in a row of wardrobes. On the floor in front of them were various items he had discarded, or changed his mind about.

I looked out of his bedroom window, out over his back lawns. All very quiet and peaceful – except that at the end of his garden, about 50 metres away, was the rear of another house, with a window clearly overlooking his bedroom window.

That must be annoying, I said, people able to see straight into your bedroom, when you are sleeping, or whatever.

'Don't talk about it. I'd never realised that. I don't think I'll be staying ...'

I'd caught him on a bad day. Tired and also pretty fed up, for some reason I never fathomed. As John Gregory had said, he can go down, when everything in his life is not as he wants it. And living on his own can't help much, except that he didn't appear unhappy on his own, didn't moan about it, or regret it, appearing self sufficient, enclosed, contained.

But football wise, things were getting pretty tense, now that the season was coming to an end, with the possibility of three trophies. Perhaps that was it. He'd flown through the season so far, scoring freely, fitting in marvellously, loved by all. Now things were getting serious.

Match One:
The Premier League Title,
16 May 1999.

Manchester United   vs.   Tottenham

Manchester United	Tottenham
1. Peter Schmeichel	1. Ian Walker
2. Gary Neville	2. Stephen Carr
3. Denis Irwin	12. Justin Edinburgh
4. David May	4. Steffen Freund
5. Ronny Johnsen	17. John Scales
16. Roy Keane	23. Sol Campbell
7. David Beckham	24. Tim Sherwood
18. Paul Scholes	18. Steffen Iversen
19. Dwight Yorke	9. Darren Anderton
10. Teddy Sheringham	10. Les Ferdinand
11. Ryan Giggs	14. David Ginola

Substitutes

8. Nicky Butt (18) 70	13. Espen Baardsen
9. Andy Cole (10) h-t	20. Jose Dominguez (14) 10
12. Phil Neville (11) 80	22. Andy Sinton (20) 78
17. Raimond Van Der Gouw	25. Stephen Clemence
20. Ole Gunnar Solskjaer	32. Luke Young (17) 71

We're supposed to take the day before a match very quietly and rest a lot. As it was a home game, the routine was like that for an ordinary League match.

But of course it wasn't an ordinary League match. We had to beat Spurs in order to win the League. Arsenal were just one point behind, and playing at the same time. Against Villa, as it happens. If we lost or drew, and Arsenal won, Arsenal would retain the Premiership title. The day before we did some light training then I came home and went to bed, dozed for two or three hours. I often do that in the afternoons. I don't like going out between 3.30 and 6.00 anyway. I hate the traffic. So I'm always in my house.

On Sunday morning my body clock woke me between 8.00 and 8.15 as it always does. I stayed in bed, trying to get some more sleep. Then I had some orange juice and a yoghurt. I never drink tea or coffee. Never have done. I don't like the taste. If I'm in company, trying to be sociable, in someone's house, I might, if pushed. But I'd never ask for it. I much prefer cold drinks. I suppose it's being brought up in the West Indies.

I messed around then left for Old Trafford about 12.30 in my Ferrari. We get it parked for us on match days. It only takes me about half an hour to get there, so I was there at one o'clock – three hours before a game. That's what we're supposed to do.

There were the usual hundreds of people wanting autographs – and I signed what seemed like hundreds. It's very rarely I refuse, though it can take up so much time.

I went into reception, said hi to all the girls, signed a few shirts and photos for charity, and went upstairs.

We always have a meal together in a dining room. It's always pasta. I drink lime and lemonade with it. Then I had rice pudding afterwards. Just the normal pre-match meal. Some of them eat huge amounts. I can't believe it. Oh they know who they are. OK then, Becks, Giggsy, Butty, Coley. You should see what they put away.

Then we went into the players' lounge, messed around, watched TV. Before a match, friends and relations aren't allowed in the players' lounge, only after the match.

At 2.30 we had the team meeting, with the Gaffer taking us through things. He has a board on a wall, moving players around on magnet things. It's all very organised and spot on, always straight to the point. After all, he's been doing it for years.

He took a bit longer than usual – 30 minutes as opposed to 20. He sort of reiterated things we knew we had to do. We all knew how important it was. But he still had to take us through it.

Until the team talk, we don't know the team, though we

always get vibes, or think we do. We all look for clues. I had a feeling Andy wouldn't play, but I didn't know whether Teddy or Ole would play instead. Andy had vibes that he wouldn't be starting.

It's normal, till we're told, to try and work it out. I don't usually get it right. Sometimes I don't even come close.

Do I always feel confident I'll be in? Hmm. I suppose I do. Otherwise I would be having negative thoughts, wouldn't I, and that's bad. So no. I had no negative thoughts about not being in the team that day.

During the season, I had only been left out twice – and I was told why by the Gaffer. He said I needed a rest. With the squad we have, no one can expect to play every game.

In the team talk, he did deal with Spurs, told us to give them respect, to watch Ginola. We knew that Ferdinand was playing, and we know he's good in the air, so he went over what to do with him. We were all pumped up, so there was no need really to tell us too much.

No, no one nods off in team talks, or looks bored, even in a long one. No one would do that ...

Over lunch I sat beside Becks and Teddy, going over the possible scores – in our game and the Arsenal game. Anything is possible in football. You can always be surprised. Someone said Arsenal could beat Villa 3–0. We all said we didn't care about that. A win by 1–0 would do us. We'd settle for that.

After the team talk, we put in time watching TV in the players' lounge. It was the Grand Prix and several were watching that.

I don't have any dressing-room superstitions. I'm just not superstitious. Well, apart from always trying to be last out. I always was at Villa. Coming to Manchester United, I found that Andy Cole likes to be last out. Normally we sort of joggle for it, one trying to get behind the other as we stand in the tunnel. Sometimes we come out together. With this match, with Andy not starting, I was able to be last out.

My lycra shorts under my shorts are not a superstitious thing. I've done that for years. It just sort of feels more comfortable.

Wearing my collar up, well that started many years ago.

Nothing to do with coming to Manchester United and trying to look like Cantona. Though I did start doing it because of watching Cantona with his collar up. I thought that looks cool.

The bit of plaster on my left hand, covering the two middle figures, yeah, that's a recent thing. But it's not a fashion thing. No, it's not to cover my ring. I take that off in the dressing room. The plaster is to protect this finger. It's begun to get sore in recent matches, with being whacked all the time. It keeps on hurting when I'm tackled. I don't know why. But it's been killing me. So I now cover it with a bit of plaster, to protect it. Don't think it's arthritis. Dunno what it is. I haven't seen a doctor. Why should I?

Once on the pitch, I did my usual thing. I touch the grass then touch my body, in the sign of the cross. I always have done. It's the last thing I always do, before every game ...

Watching the match, most fans were not surprised to see Sheringham playing instead of Cole. The newspapers had predicted it, either from hints from Fergie, or just good guesswork.

But I was surprised to see Roy Keane in the team. He had been injured, so we'd been led to believe. Fergie, as Hoddle did, tends to be economical with the truth about injuries. Jaap Stam was out with an injury. David May was playing.

I am a Spurs fan, always have been, so it was a hard game to watch, emotionally, not just because I wanted Dwight, my new best friend, to do well, but because all Spurs supporters were a bit ambivalent about what sort of result we wanted. A Spurs win could make Arsenal top of the League, once again. Did we want that? Did we heckers. The joke in North London all week had been that Spurs, to make it really really hard for Manchester United, were going to put Dominguez in goal.

Spurs started well, more aggressive and determined, but Dwight had a half chance in the fourth minute, easing a cross from Giggs towards the Spurs goal, but Walker saved it. Dwight had an even better chance, minutes later, when he put pressure on Walker who was taking his time over a kick. An old and highly irritating habit of Walker's, which we thought George Graham had cured. When he finally kicked the ball, it hit Dwight, just yards away by now. It trickled towards goal, appeared to be going in, then hit the post and rebounded. Lucky Walker. Hard cheese Dwight.

Around the ten-minute mark, Ginola was injured and came off. He had been voted Footballer of the Year by both the Professional Footballers' Association and the Football Writers' Association. Mainly for some exceptional goals earlier in the season. Dwight was runner-up.

In the 18th minute, Dwight had a third half chance. He managed a shot, from an acute angle, which went across the goal, ending up near the corner flag.

Manchester United were by now getting a grip, taking control, while Spurs with Dominguez on instead of Ginola didn't look much of a threat. Football being football, Spurs then scored. In the 25th minute, Iversen headed on a long ball from Walker to Ferdinand. He steadied himself and before Ronny Johnsen could get in a tackle, he chipped the ball over Schmeichel and into the net. One–nil to the Littlewhites.

Manchester United then re-doubled their efforts, but Walker was in excellent form. In the 36th minute, Dwight had another half chance, which he tried to steer in with his left foot. Walker saved.

Then in the 42nd minute, David Beckham scored. It was Manchester United's first clear-cut chance, as opposed to half chances. Scholes won it in midfield from Tim Sherwood, which some Spurs players thought was a foul. Scholes ran on and fed it to Beckham on the right of the penalty area. He stayed calm, shooting over Walker in the far left-hand corner of the net. So 1–1 at half time. At Highbury it was 0–0.

Andy Cole came on for Sheringham at the start of the

second half and in two minutes had scored. From then on, Manchester United were totally in charge, yet unable to score a third goal and make the game safe. At 2–1, Spurs could easily equalise, just as easily as they'd got their first goal.

News came through that Arsenal were one goal up, which made the Manchester United fans decidedly jittery. Spurs could well nick a goal, and let Arsenal in to win the championship.

Manchester United continued to have all the chances, and Spurs the odd breakaway. But Manchester United comfortably managed to hang on. They won 2–1. And the championship. So how was the game for you, Dwight?

When we were missing chance after chance, I thought it's going to be one of those days. Then when Scholes sent one over the bar, that was worrying. He's the best finisher in training.

When Ferdinand scored, I squatted down in the centre circle. You probably didn't notice. I felt we were in total control, then that happened. Oh no, I thought, what's going on.

Then I thought, we've enough talent in this team, we'll have to keep going. The thing about Manchester United is that over the years, they always keep going.

When Becks scored, I thought that's it, we'll get three or four now. We do seem to do best when we're chasing the game. I think the fear factor goes when you need a result, when you just have to score. So at half time, when it was 1–1, I felt very much better.

In the dressing room at half time, I could hear the Gaffer shouting at some people. Not at me. I don't know who. I had my head in a towel. I was so hot. He was shouting about something that had gone wrong. Then he told Andy to get changed. Teddy's expression was not a happy one, but the Gaffer explained to him what he was doing. I thought Teddy had been doing well, getting it in the air, flicking it on.

If I got pulled off, and didn't agree with it, I wouldn't complain, not there and then. At the age of 27, I know it's better to wait till you've calmed down. But after two days I would, if the team had lost and I still couldn't understand it, I'd ask for an explanation.

But when Andy came on, it all clicked. So the Gaffer's sitting there, well pleased. He's pulled it off again. If he hadn't, Teddy would have had a good case to complain. But when the team wins, you can't say much, can you?

So yeah, when that final whistle blew, it was brilliant. I knew at last what it's like to be at the top ...

There was immediately mass cuddling among the Manchester United players, with Dwight being the most cuddled, the most joyous. His natural expression, all things being equal, is to look joyous, but this was mega joy, mega happiness. He had of course never won the League Championship before. For Fergie and many of his players, it was their fifth triumph, though the first to be clinched at home at Old Trafford.

Dwight had what appeared to be a golden crown on his head, the top part of the championship cup. The music was triumphant, blasting out their victory. Overhead an aeroplane appeared, trailing behind a banner with the legend 'MUFC Carling Champions, 98–99'. Down at Highbury, had they got another banner ready, with Arsenal's name on it?

It was Peter Schmeichel's last league game for Manchester United. He appeared to be in tears when Fergie said he was the best goalie he had ever seen. Then Schmeichel said Fergie was the best manager in the history of the universe. Or words to that effect. Schmeichel brought his three children on to the pitch for a photo opportunity. Andy Cole brought on his child.

Jaap Stam, who had not played, but sat in the dugout in a suit, appeared in full strip to collect his winner's medal, wearing a red, black and white wig. Dwight had acquired a black baseball cap, with the Carling logo on. Wearing it back to front, of course. As he lifted up the cup and crown, for the umpteenth time, he let the crown fall to the ground.

A banner in the crowd said, 'Goodbye Peter Thank You.' Another said, 'Now Let the Fat Lady Sing.'

The latter, presumably, was to let us know it wasn't all over. One title down. Still two to go ...

Match 2:
The FA Cup Final,
22 May 1999.

Manchester United	vs.	Newcastle United
1. Peter Schmeichel		13. Steve Harper
2. Gary Neville		38. Andrew Griffin
12. Phil Neville		16. Laurent Charvet
4. David May		4. Didier Domi
5. Ronny Johnsen		34. Nikos Dabizas
16. Roy Keane		12. Dietmar Hamann
7. David Beckham		7. Robert Lee
18. Paul Scholes		24. Nolberto Solano
9. Andy Cole		9. Alan Shearer
20. Ole Gunnar Solskjaer		14. Temuri Ketsbaia
11. Ryan Giggs		11. Gary Speed

Substitutes

6. Jaap Stam (18) 76		1. Shay Given
10. Teddy Sheringham (16) 9		2. Warren Barton
15. Jesper Blomqvist		10. Silvio Maric (24) 68
17. Raimond Van Der Gouw		17. Stephen Glass (14) 78
19. Dwight Yorke (9) 60		20. Duncan Ferguson (12) h-t

Newcastle United were back at Wembley for the Cup Final, as they had been the previous year against Arsenal. Once again, it mattered. They had nothing else to cheer themselves up, having had another disappointing season. Most people, including the bookies, saw them as the underdogs, with little chance.

And yet on ITV, the two studio pundits, Terry Venables and John Barnes, both predicted a Newcastle win. Strange predictions, when Manchester United had not been beaten for 32 games and Newcastle had not won a game for 41 days. Venables did say, however, that Dwight Yorke had been his personal player of the year.

Whatever happened, the winner would be United. Now that was strange. There are 15 Uniteds amongst the 92 teams in the Football League, and yet in this 118th FA Cup Final, it was the first time two Uniteds had met in the final.

For anoraks everywhere, the 15 Uniteds, in order of age, are: Sheffield 1889; Newcastle 1892; West Ham, 1900; Manchester, 1902; Carlisle, 1903; Southend, 1906; Hartlepool, 1908; Scunthorpe, 1910; Leeds, 1919; Torquay, 1921; Rotherham, 1925; Peterborough, 1934; Colchester, 1937; Cambridge 1949; Oxford, 1960.

When Manchester United's team was announced there was one big surprise – Dwight Yorke was not playing. The *Daily Telegraph* had suggested as much, also saying Giggs would not play. The thinking was that Fergie wanted to rest both, keeping them fresh for the Champions' League final. They got it half right. Giggs did play, but Solskjaer played up front with Cole, instead of Dwight.

My first reaction was that Dwight was exhausted by all the celebrations after the League Championship win. I saw him during the week and he hadn't been at his home for three nights. On the night of the win, all the Manchester United players had gone to an official celebration dinner at the Motram Park hotel.

Some of them went into town afterwards for a drink, then came back to the hotel. Dwight didn't get to bed till five o'clock. He just stayed at the hotel. Next day, in the evening, they all went for a 'boys' night' into town.

That was the evening Roy Keane was accused of hitting

a woman in a bar. Dwight says it was nothing really, just what happens when you play for Manchester United. You get followed and hassled by people. They were perfectly happy on their own and didn't want people barging in.

According to a barman, two women approached Roy, asked for a drink, then started making remarks. That's when he allegedly pushed one away. He was arrested and spent the night in police cells. He was visited at 9.15 next morning by Alex Ferguson.

Heh ho. That's football. In the end, the charge was dropped, but it had made it a tiresome and tiring week in which to prepare for the Cup Final.

Roy Keane recovered enough from his ordeal to be included in the Manchester United team. As was Paul Scholes. It was going to be their last match of the season, as each was suspended for the final European match to come.

The VIPs at Wembley included Prince Charles, there to present the Cup, and two prime ministers, each of whom, one might have thought, would have had mightier topics to take up their time and thoughts. Tony Blair, the UK Prime Minister, was there with Bertie Aherne, the Irish Taoiseach. The Irish talks, that day, were hanging in the balance, but then they had been, almost every day. An FA Cup Final comes only one day a year. They kindly gave us their considered thoughts on the match to come.

Mr Blair, though born in Scotland, was brought up in Durham and considers the north east his home region, and it is where the seat of his constituency is. He looks upon Newcastle as his home team. (One of his sons follows Manchester United, while the other supports Liverpool, Cherie Blair's home town.)

Mr Aherne supports Manchester United, one of those thousands of fanatical Irish fans who rarely see them play in the flesh. He appeared highly knowledgeable, listing all the teams Manchester United had beaten on the way to the Final. When asked to predict, Mr Aherne said his team was not as strong as he would have liked. Mr Blair giggled when asked for his comments. At last year's Final, he said, Newcastle had played poorly, but he was sure this time they would play much better. Roughly what Barnes and Venables thought.

Newcastle started at full pelt, charging into Manchester United, chasing every ball, upending players, lashing out, determined to upset Manchester United before they could settle. A reasonable tactic, given that Manchester United had the better and more skilful players.

The result was that after only eight minutes Roy Keane was off, his ankle injured in a tackle. There was no obvious substitute as Butt was not on the bench, so on came Teddy Sheringham. Within two minutes, he had scored. It was the prettiest move of the match, which Sheringham himself had begun.

Sheringham had two other chances, both headers, while Cole nearly scored, but the match was becoming scrappy. The only real patterns to be seen were some complicated diamond and diagonal shapes created on the turf by the Wembley groundsman.

After half time, Duncan Ferguson came on for Newcastle in place of Hamann. Just when Newcastle appeared to be finding a bit of steam, Manchester United scored again. Sheringham laid a ball back to Scholes who scored cleanly.

On the hour mark, I could see Dwight being told to get stripped off. As he stood, ready to come on, he was signing autographs. I hoped Fergie didn't notice, or he might get a bollocking.

Dwight came on for Andy Cole and was immediately presented with what looked like a fairly good chance from a cross by Giggs. He headed it wildly over the bar. He had another reasonable chance a few minutes later, but passed to someone else instead of shooting.

The game ended 2–0 to Manchester United. Sheringham was deservedly judged Man of the Match by

Ron Atkinson on ITV. Fergie hugged Keane, his captain, who had played only the smallest part. The team did a huddle of triumph in the centre circle, reminiscent of the New Zealand rugby team.

Compared with the Premiership win, six days earlier, the celebrations were muted. Even Dwight was relatively restrained, but then he had not played the full game. Several Manchester United players had been suffering from flu in the last few days, notably Gary Neville, whose eyes were narrow, his face flushed.

Alan Shearer, ever the sporting Englishman, was about the only Newcastle player on his feet and watching when Manchester United went up the steps to accept the FA Cup. He even managed a relatively hearty clap. Tony Stephens must have been proud of him.

I had no idea I wasn't going to play until the morning of the match, no idea at all.

We travelled down to London by coach and as usual I played cards all the way – with Roy, Denis Irwin and the Gaffer. Oh yeah, the Gaffer loves his cards. We play 13-card brag. For money of course, but not much, just £20 a time. On a good day, I might win £300. Or I might lose it. We pay up, there and then, or later. If it's later, Roy will soon let you know if you owe him money. I always played cards at home in Tobago. I still do, when I'm with my friends.

We stayed the night at a hotel. Can't remember the name. I rarely do. Life as a footballer is constantly moving into hotels. It's all done for you, the booking in, everything. You go up to your room, you come down, you go to eat, you might as well be anywhere. Often when I ring a girl or a friend, I have no idea where I am. I can't tell people where I'm staying.

I'm always in a single room. Have been for years. Once I became a senior player at Villa, a regular in the first team, I asked for a single room. That's what I prefer. I did share when I was younger, but not now. Several other of the Manchester United players prefer to be alone, such as Becks and Schmeichel.

How I prepare the night before a match is different from my team mates, so I wouldn't want to upset or annoy them. I often don't get to bed till 2.00 a.m. I might then get up, have a drink, watch the television or ring people all over the world. That's normal for me. That's why I want a single room. I hope I'll always get it, unless the chairman says I can't have one.

Anyway, the Gaffer knocked at my door at 10.00 in the morning. This is what he does, on match days, if he wants to warn someone privately, in advance, about what he's going to do. We all know about 'the knock'.

It was the first time it's happened to me, since I joined Manchester United. I had been on the bench against Chelsea, but then I was being rested. He'd told me that in training, well ahead, that he was resting me.

When he told me I wasn't starting in the FA Cup Final, I said you must be joking. I could not believe it. I said I want to play. It's what I've come to Manchester United to do, to play in big matches like these.

His explanation was that he didn't want me to get injured. I was one of his ace cards for Wednesday in Barcelona.

No, he never mentioned anything about thinking I was tired. That was his explanation – he didn't want me to get injured. I argued that he had to play his best team, not think of injuries.

But what could I do, what else could I say? I certainly didn't feel at all tired. There had been no signs at all of tiredness. So I just had to accept it.

I suppose if I had to miss one of the big three matches, that was the one to miss, not the Bayern one. But I wanted to play in all three. It was a big blow. I was very disappointed.

At the team meeting, when he officially told us all the team, I was hurt even more. Becks and Giggs were both playing – yet they are key players as well, his ace cards. And Coley was playing as well. It was as close to his first team as it could be, apart from me, and apart from those injured.

Teddy wasn't in the team either. He looked at me across the room and gave me a shrug, made a face. I suppose he was surprised I wasn't in the team – he expected me to play.

But you can't knock the Gaffer. All season he has made changes – and he's been right. It's impossible to complain, not afterwards, when he's been proved right. You argue with him, at the time, and I'm sure he expects that. He'd want you to argue and be upset. But then you have to accept it. When he left my room, having told me, he said, 'Trust me. We'll win ...'

It was awful in the dressing room before the match, knowing I wasn't starting, trying not to look too fed up, trying to keep my face. And sitting on the bench was awful as well. But you are part of the team, you have to do your best for the team as a whole.

I was gutted when Skip got injured. Keano has been one of the top boys of the season, a very influential player. He already knew he was going to miss the Bayern game. And he'd an awful week, with the night in gaol. Terrible. Yet he was so brave.

When he came off, he sat beside me on the bench. I asked him what was wrong, which tackle had done it. Yeah, Newcastle had started very hard. That was their intention, to upset our rhythm. I put an arm round his shoulder, said it could be worse, that sort of thing.

At half time, I felt confident we would win. The first 20 minutes had been hard, but when the other team tires, we always come into our own. I could see them already getting tired.

In the dressing room, the Gaffer said they had to pass and move, not run around, because the ground was sticky.

The Gaffer sat down next to Blomqvist, so I thought he might be coming on for the second half. But he didn't make any changes.

After ten minutes of the second half, he told me to get ready, I was coming on.

Yeah, I was signing a few autographs at the time. In fact most of the time I was on the bench. But I was sat behind the Gaffer, so he couldn't see. People just kept passing things over, saying oh go on, please sign. I don't like refusing. No, I don't think it spoiled my concentration. I felt lovely. There were no butterflies in my stomach. I never feel nervous beforehand.

That header that went over, well, it did arrive too high for me. But I felt confident. No problems. I felt in control.

Perhaps the excitement afterwards was not the same as winning the Premiership. That was bigger in a way, being the first one.

That evening we had a club celebration dinner in London, at the Royal Lancaster. For the players, wives, girlfriends, officials. I got to bed about 4.00 in the morning.

Next day, on Sunday afternoon, we did some light training at Bisham Abbey. By chance, I met Andy Comyn there, my old room mate from Sheila's. I'm not sure what he was doing there.

So we only had one evening celebrating the FA Cup win. We knew we had to eat right, stay right, come down quickly from winning the Double.

We all knew the really big one was to come. We didn't have to be reminded that we could now win the Treble ...

Match Three:
European Champions' League Final
Wednesday, 26 May 1999.

Manchester United	vs.	Bayern Munich
1. Peter Schmeichel		1. Oliver Kahn
2. Gary Neville		2. Markus Babbel
3. Denis Irwin		18. Michael Tarnat
15. Jesper Blomqvist		4. Samuel Osei Kuffour
5. Ronny Johnsen		25. Thomas Linke
6. Jaap Stam		16. Jens Jeremies
7. David Beckham		14. Mario Baster
8. Nicky Butt		21. Alexander Zickler
9. Andy Cole		19. Carsten Jancker
19. Dwight Yorke		10. Lothar Matthäus
11. Ryan Giggs		11. Stefan Effenberg

Substitutes	*Substitutes*
4. David May	5. Thomas Helmer
10. Teddy Sheringham (15) 67	7. Mehmet Scholl (21) 71
12. Phil Neville	8. Thomas Strunz
17. Raimond Van Der Gouw	17. Thorsten Fink (10) 80
20. Ole Gunnar Solksjaer (9) 81	20. Hasan Salihamidzic (14) 88
30. Wesley Brown	22. Bernd Dreher
34. Jonathan Greening	24. Ali Daei

We flew out on Concorde to Barcelona on the Monday at two o'clock, after some light training in the morning. Yeah, on Concorde. The Gaffer had told us about it a few days earlier. It was like winning another medal. I hadn't been on it before, and I don't think most players had. Apart from Becks. He might have been. I'd heard so much about it, so I knew it was quite small inside. But not that small. It was brilliant. And the food was exquisite. It went even faster than my Ferrari ...

At Barcelona, there was a huge crowd of Manchester United fans, waiting for us. Our hotel was about 45 minutes away. No idea where, or its name. But it was nice enough.

At 11.30 the next morning, the Tuesday, we all went for a walk, all together. Then we had the team meeting. The Gaffer said I was playing – but I knew that already. Before the Cup Final, he had made that clear. He was saving me for this one.

The team was pretty obvious, given that there was no Keano or Scholes. Teddy was upset, but it was expected that me and Coley would be up front. Teddy had done well in recent games, but all season, my partnership with Coley had been so good. I don't think any of the lads were surprised.

That night, Tuesday, the night before the game, I had an awful sleep. I don't know what was wrong. I just had a terrible dream. It's unusual for me, having bad dreams. It woke me up, about 2.00, so I switched on the TV, trying to get something in English. I'd already watched Sky News about 100 times that evening, but I couldn't find it. All I could find was something in Spanish, so I watched that, without knowing a word.

I rang a friend in Australia, but couldn't get through. I sat and thought, now who else can I ring at this time of night? I couldn't think of anyone. So eventually I went back to bed, but I didn't sleep well. I honestly can't remember the dream. I'm not sure if you would call it a nightmare. I can't remember. I was with a woman, yeah. No, it wasn't unpleasurable, but it ended suddenly and I woke up. No, it's gone. Can't remember.

Next morning, the Gaffer said to me and Gary Neville that we would be taking questions at the press conference. It was mega. I thought my first press conference, when I signed for Manchester United, was big, but this was enormous. Oh, well over 100 journalists, from all over. The questions were OK – what was the mood in the camp, were we confident – normal questions, and I gave normal answers.

I don't mind doing them, they're not a problem. But I'm now getting to the stage when I'd rather not. I'd rather have a break and let someone else do them. I'd prefer to be left alone, just get on with playing football, concentrate on that, not to talk to journalists. Let them write what they want. I don't read the papers anyway. So I don't care what they write.

When we got to the Nou Camp, you just stand there, looking up at the stands and think bloody hell, it's unbelievable. I'd been there once before, when we played Barcelona. And I thought the same thing – fantastic.

The atmosphere in the dressing room was fine. Cool, quiet, but I'd say quite relaxed. We have been through pressure matches before. It wasn't exactly a new scene for us.

The press and pundits were not so sure about who would start. Some thought Sheringham must be in, as he had done so well in the two previous games, coming good, or at least coming on positively from the benches after another season being partially sidelined. In that case, would Yorke or Cole be sub? Neither had appeared to be in top form, so some maintained.

But of course there was no need to drop either, after such a season. The need was to compensate for Keane and Scholes, out through suspension. In came Blomqvist and Butt, with Beckham detailed to play in the middle, in Keane's position, directing play. A bit of a chance, that, bit of a gamble, not having Beckham doing what Beckham had been doing all season.

In the German team at kick off were ten German players. Worth mentioning, because elsewhere in planet football, such a thing rarely happens these days. In the English team were only four English players – Beckham, Butt, Cole and Gary Neville. The other seven came from Denmark, Holland, Norway, Sweden, Eire, Wales and Tobago. Also of interest was the fact that the captain of each team that evening was their goalkeeper.

Manchester United were in red, having won the toss for strips, a good omen, so all Red Devils were thinking.

Schmeichel started nervously, making a couple of wild clearances with his left foot which went into touch. A bad omen, so Red Devils tried to stop themselves from thinking. Nor did he appear to be shouting and commanding, which was worrying, considering all the big games he had played in since joining Manchester United in 1991.

Bayern started confidently, solid and organised, without showing much creatively or causing any danger, but it was early doors, as Big Ron might say. Still very early doors, in fact only the fifth minute, when Ronny Johnsen gave away a free kick on the edge of the Manchester United penalty area. It looked harmless enough, both the alleged foul and the situation. Except that Bayern scored. A Bayern player appeared to pull Butt to one side, letting the ball through the wall, and Schmeichel hardly moved. Keane, if he'd been there, would surely have organised them better.

A terrible mistake, a terrible beginning, but one which Manchester United had grown used to overcoming, as in the Spurs game ten days earlier.

As the match progressed, Bayern appeared not just to be solid and organised, but growing bigger, especially the towering figure of Jancker up front. Manchester United, apart from Stam, seemed weedy by comparison, missing Keane's physical aggression and menace. Beckham, despite all his talents, isn't exactly a Vinnie Jones. Yorke and Cole were being pushed out of it, their first touches poor, when they did get any chances, which was rare, though Dwight did have a hooked shot over his shoulder which went wide.

More worrying was Manchester United's body language, with players shouting at each other, appearing confused by their own tactics and formation. Giggs was also playing out of position, to let Blomqvist have the left wing. Nothing was flowing, nothing happening for them. Bayern seemed content to contain them.

In the 66th minute, Sheringham came on for Blomqvist. It didn't make much difference. Bayern had moved on from containment to confidence, beginning to make dangerous breakaways. In the 78th minute, they hit the post, after the best move of the match so far. Cole then gave way to Solskjaer, but Bayern still looked more likely to score, despite some good saves from Schmeichel. With seven minutes to go, Bayern hit the woodwork for the second time. Dwight had a modest chance, but miscued. On realistic chances made, a fair score would now be 3–0. As the 90th minute was reached, it was still 1–0 to Bayern. That seemed that.

Manchester United had not been beaten in 33 games. A record that was there, waiting to be broken. They had made a habit of coming back from behind, but again, we all know that can't go on.

In injury time, Manchester United got a corner which Beckham took. Schmeichel rushed up, hoping for a touch, to get in the way, for anything really, just to go out still trying. The ball came out to Giggs, who mishit his shot, but it ran to Sheringham, half with his back to goal, who steered it into the net.

Bloody lucky, was my first thought. Can't call it a miracle. Miracles are usually deserved. But it was a reprieve, if only temporary, for surely Bayern will win in extra-time, having clearly been the better team.

Before I'd got my mind round the thought of extra time, trying to remember if it would be golden goals and sudden death or whatever, a second dollop of bloody luck landed at Manchester United's feet. From another corner, Sheringham headed it on towards goal. Solskjaer stuck out a foot and poked it home. Two goals in two minutes of injury time. Must be a miracle now. No other word for it. The Bayern players were on the ground, disbelieving, horrified. The referee had to help them up – only to blow the whistle.

Even the Manchester United players seemed in shock, dazed and confused. Their emotions, settled into the acceptance of defeat, had been churned up, chopped up, chucked in the air and hadn't quite come down.

Their goal in six minutes was a terrible blow. I couldn't believe it. It was nothing new, as we'd gone through the Championship chasing games, having to fight back from being behind. But it was very disappointing.

Yes, there was a bit of shouting at each other, but there always is, when you concede a goal. Players say 'Why didn't you clear it, why didn't you do this or that?' Pete never has anyone on the line for free kicks. He's so good. He doesn't need them. So I don't know what happened, how it got through the wall.

But you do what you always do – think positive. You have to think ahead, tell yourself there are still 80 minutes to go, we can still get back.

But as the game went on, I have to admit I didn't see it coming. It wasn't a classic game. We didn't play as well as we can. No, I'm not saying I personally didn't play well. You don't think that, at the time.

I felt great during the game, no problems. But sometimes, when you are trying to be a hero, so eager to score the winning goal, it just doesn't work out. You have already played the game in your mind. Then when you get out there, you're thinking, 'If ever I want it to go well, this is the time, this is the one.' Then if it doesn't go well, well, things get worse.

People said afterwards we didn't play as well as we did in Turin. That's true. People also said we missed Keano and Scholes. I don't know. But during the game, I felt fine. I wasn't aware of playing any different from usual.

As it got near the end, I did think that was it. At the 90th minute, I thought we couldn't come back now. Not this time. It's too late. No one watching could have thought we would do it. Nor did we. We were dead and buried.

That didn't mean we gave up, whatever was in our minds. That's not the Manchester United way. You might have doubts. But you don't give up.

I wasn't aware that the referee had given four minutes of injury time. Or was it three? I didn't see the board.

All I knew was that it was the 90th minute and we'd got a corner. I saw Pete coming up. He got a touch, yes he did, because I saw it. Then I headed it back towards the goal.

When Teddy scored, I thought now we'll be having extra time proper. We've saved ourselves, just in time. Now for extra time.

The second goal was pure shock. I hadn't believed we would draw level, so when we scored again, it was just well, another shock.

One moment I was feeling so disappointed. It was the big occasion, the one we'd waited so long for, and we hadn't pulled it off. That was still in my mind. I'd got used to feeling that feeling, that we were out. The next moment was this enormous relief. But it all happened so quickly. I just felt stunned.

We had a reception afterwards, a buffet affair, for the club and everyone, like our FA Cup Final dinner, with wives and girlfriends. I had no girlfriend there of course, but Jordi Cruyff [a Manchester

United player, then on loan to Celta Vigo] had already been in touch with me beforehand. So I went out with him, into Barcelona, plus two of his friends. We were in a nightclub, dancing and enjoying ourselves. I didn't get back to the hotel till 9.00 in the morning. It was a tremendous evening.

We flew back to Manchester later in the day. Not Concorde this time. Monarch. Not quite the same. At Manchester Airport they had a red carpet laid down to greet us.

Then we had the procession through the streets. I've never seen such crowds. In Deansgate, it was unbelievable. Players who had won the Double said they'd seen nothing like this. All these hundreds and thousands, looking up at us on the coach. You just wanted to thank them back, for what they'd given us.

You noticed the cigar, did you? No, I wasn't smoking it. I never smoke. What happened was that Pete Schmeichel was ordering some cigars for after the match, so I said get one for me, the biggest Havana you can get.

He gave it to me in Barcelona, after the match. I took it with me to the nightclub and had it in and out of my mouth all evening. Not smoking. Just posing with it.

By the time we were on the coach, it was already getting in a mess, putting it in and out of my mouth. It was starting to disintegrate. In the end, it just fell to pieces. Sort of disappeared.

No, I don't know why it appealed to me. It gave me a buzz, putting a cigar in my mouth. Where I come from, the image of smoking a big cigar is that you are now successful. So that was it, I suppose.

Next morning was brilliant. Waking up thinking, ah, no training today. It's all over, for another season.

I can now go and see Brian, playing cricket for the West Indies at Old Trafford. Then I can go home to Tobago, and relax ...

Part 4
TOBAGO

38 In Tobago, when I finally caught up with Dwight, or at least he caught up with me, I put it to him that there had perhaps been a subliminal message in his cigar. It wasn't just that he was signalling he was now a success but signalling where he had come from. Oh yeah, he said, how come? Because the word Tobago comes from the word tobacco. So you were holding up a symbol of your homeland. Hmm, he said.

We had planned to fly out to Tobago together, but he kept changing his plans, saying he might go to another island first with Brian Lara, then he was going to New York. I presumed that must be on Nike business. After winning the Treble, he and Tony Stephens were in negotiations with Nike as his new sponsor. The deal, depending on certain things, could bring him in £1 million a year. Strewth. What would they think of that in Tobago?

So I went ahead and booked into the Coco Reef Hotel. Dwight said he would see me there, in a day or two.

His mother Grace is still living in the same house. She refused to move when Dwight offered to buy her a bigger, smarter house. Instead, the house has been completely renovated and enlarged with a big metal security gate at the front and a new Japanese car parked at the side.

She took me round the house with pride, pointing out all the new bedrooms, the bathroom and luxury fitted kitchen done out in dark wood. We came across a workman at the back, finishing an extra shower room. The house is now more than double its orginal size with some very smart olde worlde but brand-new bow windows. More English than West Indian in style, though you do see such features all over the West Indies, as 'returnees' (those who have spent several decades living and working in the UK) come back and build their dream house.

We went into the long garden at the back where Grace still grows a few vegetables and fruit, though she hardly needs to any more, as Dwight provides for her. She pointed out her Italian basil, her lime tree and a paw paw tree. I asked about an old shack in the garden, had someone perhaps lived in it at one time. She told me to ignore it. Dwight wanted her to knock it down, but she hadn't got round to it yet.

She lives in the house with two of her nine children, sons Gary and Garth, and two of her 11 grandchildren. Gary is 33 and was inside, slumped in front of the television. I asked about his job. Grace shouted over her shoulder. 'What you does at the airport Gary?' Gary said he was a baggage handler supervisor. He has two children, but they live with the mother. The car outside was his. Bought by Dwight? No, he paid for it.

Garth, aged 31, is unmarried. He was out at work. He used to be a carpenter but now works for the council. Grace wasn't quite sure about his exact job title.

The two grandchildren who live with her are Keil, aged 12, and Osuji, aged three, children of her third daughter Deborah, who now lives in New York and works as a nursing assistant. Osuji, very bright and smiley, as a young Dwight might have looked, or so I imagined, was rushing around outside in a very expensive electric toy car. He demonstrated its reverse as well as forward gear. A present from Uncle Dwight? No, his mother bought it for him, said Grace.

I could sense that Grace still runs a pretty strict household, though the hardships are not what they were when she had nine to look after and no money. She enjoys looking after the four of them. 'Cooking and cleaning, it's what I always done.'

Juliet, her oldest child, now aged 44, lives in New York, working as a cleaner. Verlaine, 42, next in age, lives locally in Tobago and has two children. Keith, the oldest boy, aged 39, was in the police in Trinidad and is now also in New York, doing a degree in electrical engineering. He is married with three children.

Clint, aged 37, the one who was good at cricket, did become a professional cricketer, playing in England for several years. He is now a security guard in Trinidad and is married with two children. Brent, the youngest, now 25, is in the army.

Grace's children have all done well. If not quite on the scale of Dwight's doing-well. Three are now in New York, one in Trinidad, one in Cheshire. Most are married, with good jobs.

Grace has been out to see Dwight four times over the last ten years since he moved to England. She loved Birmingham. 'A very nice place, except for the cold. Sheila took me round the shops in Birmingham. I thought it was all beautiful.'

Beautiful? Birmingham? 'Yes, I bought lots of towels and sheets, but they were expensive.'

And what did she think about Sheila? 'She spoil him. She really love him, but she spoil him.'

She has been to Manchester once, last Christmas. 'I take him sorrel juice and black cake, which is what we have at Christmas.'

And his new house? Grace held her hands over her face in shock horror. 'Every bedroom, he got a television.'

And his three cars? Again her hands went up, but she made a face this time more of puzzlement than amazement.

'Dwight told me you pay less insurance, if you have three cars.' She shrugged her shoulders.

She can't quite take in Dwight's success and wealth, but then many in Britain can't either, not having got to grips with the reality of millionaire footballers. But she was very pleased, some years ago, when through Dwight she met Brian Lara's Mum.

'She same birthday as me. February 10. But she's older. She also Adventist.'

Dwight was due soon, she said, because he had rung to say so, but didn't know when. People were already coming to her front gate, distant friends but also total strangers, to ask if he had arrived yet. He would be mobbed when he did come. That always happens. She got up from the front porch and went inside to find something. She returned holding a letter and some snaps.

'This little white boy,' she said. 'He arrives at the front door with his mother. All the way from England.' She handed me the letter so I could see the address in Oxfordshire.

'He say he wanted to shake hands with the mother of Dwight Yorke. When I shake his hand, he say he's not going to wash his hands again! Look, this is him, with me. His mother took the photographs.' She'd also sent a stamped, addressed postcard of Tobago, for Grace to get Dwight to sign and send back.

I said that Dwight is famous in England. Everyone knows him for his smile. But was she, er, aware of some of the scandal stories? She said yes. They were upsetting. 'But Sheila told me they are not true. I not to believe them.' Again she shrugged her shoulders. Something else she didn't quite comprehend.

As his mother, she presumably would like to see him married and settled? 'I axe him this and he says "When the time comes". That's all I know.'

She took me into the house to admire a huge, glossy

framed photo of Dwight in his Manchester United strip. Dwight had signed it with the words, 'My Loving Mum, Lots of Love, Always, Dwight.'

Next day, I came back to see Garth, as he had been out at work. He looked a bit like Dwight, very clean, polite, charming, and extremely proud of his new job. He had trained as a carpenter then become a refrigeration technician before applying to the Council. 'I got the job on 14 September 1998. That was the day they rang me.'

As Dwight will always remember the date of the Bayern match, well if not the date, at least the day, so Garth will recall the call from the Public Health Department. To do what exactly? It's like being a health inspector, he said. He wears special protective overalls and goes round spraying houses when they have rats, roaches, mosquitoes and things. He loves it. And the wage is quite good, TT$105 [£10] a day.

He has also been to the UK with his mother. 'Dwight wanted us to fly first class, but we said no. I know he would let us have money, if we ever wanted it. We just have to ask. When I broke my leg, he paid for me to have the pin out.

'I liked Birmingham, especially the colour of the antique buildings. I went out to a nightclub with Dwight and his friends Ugo and Mark Bosnich. They were very nice to me.'

Had Dwight changed, since going to England? 'He's more disciplined, on and off the pitch. He's much stronger. He takes care of himself. He's always on time.'

How about his accent? Did he now sound different? 'Yeah, some of his friends say he now speaks like an Englishman, but back home, he speaks normal, like the other guys.'

Garth was wearing an immaculately clean Aston Villa shirt. He says he will always support Villa, even though Dwight is now at Manchester United. His other brother, Gary, however, now sports a Manchester United scarf on the front shelf of his motor car.

As we were talking, I heard the big metal gate opening and a large man in a baseball cap arrived, smoking a cigarette. Garth stood up at once, muttering that it was Fulton, his father, presumably looking to see if Dwight had arrived. Before I could stop him, Garth had scarpered inside, leaving me to explain my presence. This was my first sighting of Fulton.

I introduced myself, saying I was writing a book about Dwight, all official, with Dwight's help. He stared at me, saying nothing.

You must be proud of what Dwight has done?

'I'm proud of all my children.'

Where do you think his skill has come from?

'From God.'

He stood looking at me, defiant, hostile, clearly not wanting to talk to me. I asked where he lived, if I could come and talk to him sometime, at his convenience.

'Here and there,' he said.

So could I talk to him?

'No, I don't want to talk. Untrue tings have been said about me. Very hurtful tings.'

I took this to be a tabloid newspaper report about Dwight buying him a new £9,000 car, then quoting Fulton as saying it wasn't much.

'I never spoke to them. And I don't want to speak to you.'

He then went inside, still smoking.

I spent a lot of time trying to track down Rama, Dwight's best friend from his schooldays, the one Dwight said he would be today, but for football.

Grace said he might be at a certain playing field, but I just missed him. I called at a house and a young boy said he didn't live here. When I returned later, he was there.

Rama is 29 small, thin, very cheerful, with a big smile and a boss eye, or what was once called a boss eye.

'It happened when I was five years old. I was running

because my mother was going to beat me and I fell on a stick. My mother had said I was rude. I don't do chores.

'I was brought up by my mother. I have nine brothers and sisters on my mother's side and 14 on my father's side.'

He and Dwight played together all the time as children. Rama, being two years older, was the one who knew how to catch crabs. He still does, and brought one out of a shed to show me. His real name is Bert Benjamin, always knows as Rama.

'There was a famous gambler round here called Rama Jama. When I was young, I used to like gambling with the big guys. One of them called me Rama. It just stuck.'

He worked as a carpenter, when he left school, but now gets jobs as a labourer, when he can. 'I try to earn an honest dollar. I off today.' When in work, he makes about TT$80 [£8] a day. Which is why he still does a bit of crab catching.

Has Dwight changed?

'No, same old Dwight. Some get bigger looks when they get bigger friends. But not Dwight.

'He always had ambition. He know where he come from and he don't want to go back. He always liked. At school, girls took his books and do his school work for him.'

He isn't jealous of Dwight, as Dwight had the talent, and the breaks, which he didn't, but he is like Dwight in one respect today. 'I single man, no kids.'

Sherwin Patrick was the school goalkeeper Dwight went to live with aged 14. Unlike Rama, he has done pretty well for himself and today has his own business.

'Home Boyz', it's called. You pass it on the main road in Canaan, near where Dwight was run over. It's basically a wooden shack, but clean and brightly painted. Inside, it's a barber's shop.

Sherwin was shaving the head of a very large man, so I decided not to interrupt him till he had finished. Above the main mirror was a poster of Dwight in his Manchester United strip. On the mirror itself was written in black ink: 'NO PHUGING CREDIT.' I noted his price list which started with 'Kids Cut, $10, Mark and Shave, $10, Cut and Shave $25'.

Sherwin was in T-shirt, shorts and flip flops as he barbered away. When he'd finished, I asked what he thought of Dwight.

'Pretty all right.'

A nice, low key answer. While Dwight went off to be a footballer, Sherwin worked for an air conditioning firm then four years ago, he set himself up as a barber. Any family? 'No, I'm free, single and disengaged.'

I noticed he too had had some sort of facial injury – a deep scar on his cheek. 'I got cut with a bottle. No, not a fight. An accident,' he said, smiling. Like Rama, and Dwight, a smile always accompanied every remark.

'Dwight always told me he would make it to the top – and I would laugh. When he got the Villa trial, I didn't believe him.'

Now of course Sherwin can hardly believe what has happened to Dwight, but he was looking forward to seeing Dwight again, if and when he turned up. No, he didn't know where and when. But Dwight, when he comes, always treats his old friends and family.

39 Kenny Crooks is one of the older people in Dwight's life, who helped him along the way, rather than played with him along the way. He was and is still a teacher at Bon Accord Government School, known by school officials as BAGS.

The school is on the main road, neat and tidy, with lawns

at the front and rear. A sign on the front lawn said, 'No Walking On the Grass,' which was being totally ignored by a flock of hens. The buildings are one storey high with red tin roofs and open wire-mesh windows, as opposed to glass, to allow air to circulate.

I waited in the office of the present head, a rather stern woman in a bright red blazer who was talking to another teacher whom she had addressed on entry as 'Hello Teacher'. On the wall a faded notice listed the school rules. No fighting, no chewing gum, no weapons, all students to show a sense of decency, courtesy, good manners, honesty and pride, whether in school or not.

As I waited and the head discussed some report with the teacher, a parent burst into the office, demanding to talk to the Head. She was an attractive woman of about 30, her hair in pink curlers. Her son had been spotted in the main road, by the garage. 'What he doing out of school, in the road, at the garage.' It all came out in a torrent. The Head brought the torrent to a halt by holding up her hand. She then made the woman go slowly through the story, starting with her own name, address, job if any, which she had, her own sewing business, then her son's name, age and class.

After the mother had gone, the Head turned to me and said, 'See, that's one of the advantages of a small island. Someone always knows you, someone will always spot you.'

Just as we were about to chat, at last, another parent arrived, a man this time, much more diffident about breaking in. I said no, go ahead. He had come to put his child's name down for the school, beginning next term. The Head said, 'Fine, OK, you'll need a photograph of the child, birth certificate, immunisation form.' The man said thanks, very good of her, then departed.

He was about 100 yards down the front drive when the Head got up and shouted after him through the open door.

'I forgot one thing.'

The man turned round.

'We flog.'

Fine, said the man, he was all for flogging.

'We don't abuse,' shouted the Head. 'We flog. Is that clear?'

'No problem,' said the man.

'If you don't agree, then you'll have to find another school.'

'No, I agree, definitely,' said the man.

BAGS is the biggest primary in Tobago, as it was in Dwight's day, with 556 pupils. She had been Head for only one year but she had already made several changes, such as re-naming the three houses in the school. Formerly, they had been named after birds. Now they were named after famous ex-pupils, thus there is now Williams House, named after Dr Alison Williams who is a technical adviser to the Government; Guy House, named after Hilton Guy, Commissioner of Police; and Yorke House, named after guess who.

'Oh we are very proud of Dwight – for his speech, his deportment, his basic discipline – all of which he got here, when he was at this school. I tell every visitor that.'

Kenny Crooks was in his own classroom, and at first was not keen to talk. A feature in the British *Daily Mail* had said that some of Dwight's school friends lived in shacks, which had upset him and the local community. I said oh, the *Daily Mail*, nothing to do with me. Not mentioning of course that I have sometimes written for it.

Eventually, he was very friendly, told me all about the school teams he had looked after, the trophies he'd won and he managed to dig out photographs of a football team and a cricket team containing Dwight. He then came with me to the little photographic shop near my hotel, though school was still going on, to make sure I handed them over for copying, as I'd promised, and didn't just leave the island with them. The foreign fame of Dwight has taught

Tobagonians a weary lesson. You can't trust visiting journalists or writers.

Orville London, who taught at the two secondary schools which Dwight attended, retired from teaching four years ago at the age of 50. He's now a sports journalist and local politician, another advantage of life on a small island.

I saw him in the offices of the *Tobago News* where he is sports editor. It's only a part-time job. The paper, which is a weekly, founded in 1985, employs just one full-time journalist, the editor.

Like everyone else on Tobago, whether they are interested in football or not, Orville has followed every move in Dwight's career. Mostly they are simply cheering him on, clapping every kick, shouting out at every goal, ogling every rise in his wage packet. Quite a few have also been applauding his bedroom strike rate. Orville, however, has mainly been concentrating on Dwight's speech patterns.

'Early on in interviews, you could hear his lack of education, hear him use wrong verbs. Green verbs, we call it, when it's bad grammar. Now he speaks better English than I do.

'I am also impressed by how he copes under stress in interviews on radio and television. How he expresses himself. When he's coping well, I think, "That's our boy – scoring points at press conferences as well as goals on the pitch."

'One of the things people in Tobago don't realise is that it hasn't all come naturally. He's had to work at it. They hear about his salary and think it's all come easy. They see the end, but are not aware of the journeys he has been on to get there.'

Orville, personally, has not been too bothered by the sex-scandal stories. 'We are not prudish by nature in Tobago, unless people take advantage of other people, use their position to advantage. We also know that young men in his position get preyed upon by cynical females, and males. His exploits in the bedroom are his concern, not our concern. Our concerns are his exploits on the football pitch.'

In talking to Ken Crooks, Orville London and three or four others of the older generation for any length of time, there emerged one area of criticism. These serious-minded, mainly professional people, who helped Dwight when he was young and struggling, are now beginning to feel he should put a little more back. They say it obliquely, not wishing to be openly critical, mostly not wishing to be quoted, but it is clear how they now feel.

'There is a widespread belief that he should do something meaningful to help the island which helped him,' said Orville. 'It is something he has to address. But I am confident he will.'

On cross examination, few have worked out what this should be. Some spoke of a Trust which Dwight could endow. He could help with the new national stadium which might be named after him.

A lot of these older types are a bit saddened by what Dwight does when he is on the island, treating his old school friends and others, giving them money, taking them out, when some of them, so they say, are just layabouts, who then waste the money on frivolous things, rather than on improving themselves. They are also upset by stories of Dwight's own indulgences, such as his £150,000 Ferrari.

Whenever this topic came up, I found myself defending Dwight. In my experience of interviewing pop stars, football stars, business stars or instant lottery millionaires, especially those quite young, this is all pretty normal. Their first reaction is to help or treat their close friends, not communities or abstract concepts. They also remember the hard work they did, rather than what any officials or teachers did for them. Sometimes they are hardly aware of what was done in the background. They also object, in the case of pop stars or footballers, to being turned into role models. They didn't ask for that, don't set themselves up as that. So why should people expect it.

As for notions of a trust, Carnegies and Rockefellers and Fords didn't even think of such things when they were 27. They were still thinking of coining it in. The idea of putting back doesn't strike people till they are nearing the end of their lives or their careers. Dwight is in a profession which is short and insecure. Regardless of his fame, talent and income now, it could all come to an end next week. So that's what I told them. They didn't seem convinced.

Neil Wilson had similar thoughts when I met him, the man who was Dwight's so-called manager, who organised his Villa deal. He is still a leading businessman, on the boards of various bodies.

'Young people on this island don't have a lot of hope, so they need all the help they can get. Dwight has done well with the material things in life. Now he should also pay attention to other things in his life.'

Such as? Well, Neil was thinking of fairly simple things, like Dwight giving talks or seminars for the island's teenagers. That all takes time, organisation, I said. And anyway footballers can't plan ahead, agree to be at a certain place at a certain time. As I well know. Don't ask me.

Neil himself is still doing things for Dwight, in the sense that he has taken it upon himself to write impressive-looking reports to Government bodies, wanting Dwight honoured or recognised in some way.

Among his large mass of documents to do with Dwight, which he has written or collected over the years, was one I didn't quite believe at first, thinking it was some sort of forgery.

It's a legal document dated and signed by him and Dwight on 3 July 1991 in which it is agreed that from henceforth Neil Wilson will be Dwight's manager and agent

REPUBLIC OF TRINIDAD AND TOBAGO:

THIS AGREEMENT made this third day of July in the Year of Our Lord One Thousand Nine Hundred and Ninety-one BETWEEN **DWIGHT YORKE**, of Canaan, Tobago, (hereinafter called "the Player") of the **ONE PART** and **NEIL WILSON**, of Signal Hill, Tobago (Hereinafter called "the Manager") of the **OTHER PART**.

WHEREAS the Player is currently playing professional football in the English First Division with **Aston Villa Football Club** and is desirous of having the Manager perform functions as Manager in respect of all his professional engagements.

IT IS HEREBY AGREED that in return for services rendered as Manager, the Player will pay to the Manager a sum equivalent to 15% of all fees earned including signing-on fees and all fees from endorsements, which sum shall be exclusive of the Player's weekly wages.

SIGNED by the within-named
DWIGHT YORKE as and for his
act and deed in the presence
of:-

SIGNED by the within-named
NEIL WILSON as and for his
act and deed in the presence
of:-

in return for '15 per cent of all fees earned, including sign-ing on fees and all fees from endorsements, which sum shall be exclusive of the player's weekly wage'.

Wow. What a deal. It appeared to be an open-ended contract, to go on for ever, in which case Neil could well have made himself a small fortune. How much exactly had he earned so far?

'Not a penny. I have taken nothing from Dwight.'

So what was the point of him signing this document? 'It was in case someone unscrupulous came along and talked himself into being Dwight's agent. He would then be able to say thanks, but no thanks, I already have an agent.

I made a note to tell Tony Stephens about this deal. And watch his face.

'Funnily enough, our Inland Revenue have just heard about this agreement. They've written to ask how much income I have had from Dwight over the years. They proba-bly won't believe it when I say nothing ...'

Deborah Moore-Miggins, the lawyer who helped Neil and Dwight with his Villa contract and other documents, is still a lawyer in Tobago. She has her own successful practice and has also become a local politician. The day I met her she had just heard that she had been accepted at Harvard University to do a Master's degree. To add to her other degrees and qualifications.

She too fears that one slight drawback to Dwight's success is that some Tobagonian youths might think they don't have to stick in at school, that they can become rich and famous without passing any exams.

'Dwight is a good role model. He gives them a goal. They see that people like themselves can do it. The negative side is that they think it's easy.

It was of course her brother Wendell who was Dwight's own role model, and from her other brother that our Dwight got this name.

Both of them are now married with children and living in Florida, working as engineers. I got Wendell's telephone number in Florida and rang him.

Wendell was the star player ahead of Dwight, whom everyone, including Dwight and Bertille, thought would make it. He went to the same schools as Dwight, BAGS, Scarborough High and Signal Hill, attended Bertille's coaching clinic, had the same sort of success as Dwight in playing for the winning Intercol Cup team.

'That was in 1982, the first time we'd won it. It put Tobago on the map, made people in Trinidad notice us. And it led to my trial with Bristol Rovers.'

Dwight was lucky in that Villa, a big club, arrived out of the blue. In Wendell's case, it was a lone Englishman, an engineer, whose home was in Bristol.

'He happened to be working in Tobago and saw me play. He contacted Bertille then wrote to Rovers and recommended me and I was invited for a trial.'

There was then the problem of finding the money, but his school and others did fund raising for his airfare.

'I was there for two months. I played for the reserves and they did discuss a contract, but then I had to come home to sit my school exams. While I was away, the whole set up at the club got fired. So I was forgotten. It was harder in those days to get work permits. Anyway, it didn't work out.

'On my return, I was offered a soccer scholarship to the USA – at a University in Philadelphia. Then I went on to one in Florida. It was the same one, I think, which later offered a scholarship to Dwight. He didn't take it, because he got accepted after his Villa trial.'

Wendell got his degree in engineering. Like his sister Deborah, he is also working on a Master's. He appears settled and secure in his profession. But does he still regret at the age of 35 that he didn't make it in football?

'I see it all as a matter of destiny. Someone had to go through the rough patches to make it smoother for people who follow. I was the first from Tobago to get a soccer scholarship – and when I got there, I told them there were a hundred people back in Tobago just as good as me. Since then, dozens of people from Tobago have come to the States on soccer scholarships.

'The person who had the roughest time was Bertille. He sacrificed so much for us, though we didn't really know it at the time. He was up at 6.00 in the morning, before going to his school job, to work on his coaching clinic. He was tough, worked us real hard, but was always forgiving. He made sure we kept in line and didn't get into drugs. He did it all for us – and in the end it ruined his own marriage.

'I like to think I have given back, because I have a loving heart. You must give back. Tobago did so much for me, and for Dwight. It's not a matter of ego. God gave us talents. We have to help others. Tobago is so small, always in the shadow of Trinidad. Giving back is all we can do.'

40 After five days of expecting him every day, Dwight still hadn't turned up, then I saw him on TTT (Trinidad and Tobago Television), being interviewed, live, in Port of Spain for an hour, which was most interesting. They had some good archive videos of him playing for T and T when younger.

Then he popped up in the *Trinidad Guardian*, spread across several pages, with numerous photos, showing him at a reception with the Prime Minister, Basdeo Panday, who said that Dwight was a 'shining example of what all Trinibagonians can be.' Note the noun, a neat combination of the two islands. The Prime Minister included himself in finding Dwight a role model. 'If I were half as good a politician as you are a footballer,' he told Dwight, 'I would rule the world.'

If Dwight was half as punctual as Tony Stephens had said he now is, he would be here with me now, in Coco Reef, so I shouted back at the television and the newspapers.

He is of course the nation's star, their most famous citizen, invited everywhere, fêted and honoured. The Footballer as Hero can happen everywhere today, in big and small countries. The USA went potty about their women soccer stars. France surprised itself by going overboard about its World Cup victors. And in Carlisle, my dear, you should have witnessed the excitement when Jimmy Glass, a reserve goalkeeper no one had heard of before, scored the goal in injury time which kept Carlisle in the Third Division. Photos and souvenirs of that event are still on sale. He is back in Swindon, reserve goalkeeping, but in Carlisle, his name will live on for ever.

I wish I had been in Trinidad and Tobago during the European final in Barcelona. The streets were empty, so everyone told me, traffic ceased, with the whole nation, on both islands, glued to their TV. The agony was bad enough for normal Manchester United fans, but in Tobago, they felt their nationhood was at stake, wanting Dwight to do it for them. Then when that dramatic end arrived, everyone rushed into the streets, cars started honking, drums banging, people partying all night long.

I got the phone number for Brian Lara's mansion in Trinidad – built on land which a grateful nation had given him in honour of his cricketing achievements. I'd heard Dwight might be staying with him. He is his best friend, as he's always saying. 'I'm a Manchester United fan because my best friend plays for them. What he has achieved since arriving at Old Trafford has been magnificent. Anything I could do would pale in comparison. I'm very proud of him.'

The West Indies, cricket wise, are of course not doing so

brilliantly these days, but we won't go into that. I asked if Dwight was there and eventually he came on the phone. He said he was coming to Tobago the next day, arriving about 12.30 and would come to my hotel.

Next day I waited all afternoon, six hours in all, and still he didn't appear. Luckily I did my waiting on the hotel beach at Coco Reef, with regular rum punches to pass the time, checking for him at reception every ten minutes. And fortunately I found someone to moan at and with. Tony Francis had arrived in my hotel with a TV crew, working on a documentary for Channel Four about those best friends, Lara and Yorke.

The crew had spent three days in Trinidad, getting nowhere. They had seen and talked to Lara, but had done no filming and had failed to make contact with Dwight and were now getting pretty pissed off, having been led to believe they would get four days of filming with them, in return for a fat fee. So far, they hadn't got four minutes in the can, yet they were spending £1,000 a day, just hanging around. Not to mention all the money wasted cancelling and changing airline tickets. So it goes.

This is normal, these days, when trying to do something about superstars. 'They know there is more in it for you than them,' said Tony. 'So they can mess you about and you have to put up with it. I don't think they actually care whether our film or your book ever gets made ...' Tony old chap, another rum punch.

I did speak to Dwight, later that day, and he did apologise for not coming to my hotel. He had meant to, but things came up. He was now having dinner at his mum's, but would see me tomorrow at a house he had rented. It would be too public, staying in my hotel. Too many people.

Local radio in Tobago had been giving out announcements all week that Dwight was going to play at Shaw Park in a friendly football match the next day. Was that true? Would he turn up?

He said technically he shouldn't really. Manchester United would not be best pleased if he got injured. But with so many people now expecting it, he did hope to play, at least for a bit.

The match was to be between the Trinidad and Tobago national team and a Tobago team. And the coach of the national team was none other than Bertille St Clair. Yes, the one who did so much for Dwight's career. Another who helped along the way, Jack Warner, as President of the Trinidad and Tobago FA, has also risen up the football hierarchy. He is now a FIFA Vice President and a very important figure in world football.

You expect officials, if they are any good, to hang on and progress, but managers and coaches have shorter lives. I had presumed, before coming to Tobago, that Bertille, at the age of 58, would be retired not just from teaching but from football.

He took over the national team a year ago, having looked after various of the country's youth teams. He did retire from teaching, back in 1990, joining the Department of Sports as a coach. Under him, the senior team had been doing well and had recently beaten Cuba in the final of the Copa Caribe. That had been the reason for the Prime Minister's reception. Dwight was a guest, but had got most coverage.

Bertille is a Tobagonian, so has a house still on the island, even though he now lives on Trinidad. Next morning I went to see him. I was surprised by the size and luxuriousness of his house, with its own swimming pool and gardener strimming away.

'We have kept in touch, now and again. Dwight rang me in 1994 after he didn't make the Coca-Cola final. I told him that God has ways of testing you. When you have almost reached somewhere, that's when you have to try even harder.'

He still runs his coaching clinic in Tobago, now with 180

members, flying over from Trinidad every Saturday. 'Which costs me TT$300 each time.' It's a lot more organised now, with skill tests and certificates for graduates. Dwight once gave out the certificates, but not recently. Bertille hopes he will again, some year. His ambition for the clinic is that one day they will own their own pitch.

I asked what he thought of Dwight's £25,000 a week. Or it could be £40,000, depending on bonuses. Or £50,000, depending on rumours. Anyway, a sum with a lot of noughts at the end.

'He's worth whatever he gets because he is the best player in the world. You have to believe that, in order to succeed. I always thought Dwight would make it – but I thought others, such as Wendell, would do it before him.'

I said I had spoken to Wendell and he had told me Bertille's marriage had collapsed. He said yes. He has four children by his first marriage. Now, with a new partner, he has a little girl, Pia, aged eight.

Had he never smoked or drunk, which is what he told Dwight and the others not to do?

'I warned them not to, and I set them an example myself, but in my own hotel bedroom, I would often take a beer ...'

I'd asked because I'd noticed in a corner of his lounge his own little cocktail bar, a bit like Bryn's in Shustoke. It was decorated with football posters, flags, cups and banners presented to him by various countries and clubs.

Overall, he thought his proudest achievement as a coach was taking the nation's Under 19s team to the World Cup Finals in Portugal in 1991. 'Dwight was the captain.'

Dwight, in our long biographical chats, had not actually mentioned that to me, yet he had so clearly remembered Puerto Rico aged eight. By the time of the Under 19s, he was of course at Villa, trying to get into the first team.

'Oh we did so well, just to get there. The first time we had ever got to a world final. One of the teams we played was Australia. Bosnich was in goal for them. He brought Dwight down unfairly in the area when Dwight should have scored ...'

Oh these old scores, or lack of scores, which linger on. His face lit up when I asked if he had been to England. He went in October 1998 on a coaching course. At Lilleshall he met Graham Taylor. Naturally they talked about Dwight. Then he went to watch Dwight play for Manchester United against Everton. He was also given a conducted tour of Old Trafford. 'And do you know who took me round? Bobby Charlton.'

Sir Bobby is of course busy working for England's 2006 bid, so it's always worthwhile being kind to visiting foreigners. It was such a thrill, said Bertille, to meet one of the all-time footballing greats.

Shaw Park was jumping. People were arriving up to an hour before kick off with reggae music blaring and long queues for beer and soft drinks.

The stadium was not as primitive as I had expected, or been led to believe by Doug Ellis. He remembered it as no more than a municipal park, with only a couple of wooden benches to sit down on. It even has floodlights, though they are a fairly recent addition.

The vast majority of spectators were standing around the pitch on the grassy sides, but set back well behind one of the goals were three little wooden stands. They were all full, one of them mainly with school girls, all of them shrieking. Shaw Park is also the island's cricket ground and the scoreboard still showed the word Batsman.

By kick off, I estimated almost 5,000 were there, a huge number for a small island. They had paid TT$10 each for the privilege, so they hoped, of seeing Dwight play, in the flesh.

As I was walking round, someone shouted at me, by name, which was a surprise. It was Garth Yorke, Dwight's brother. He was holding a bottle of Carib beer, wearing shades and his Aston Villa strip, as sparklingly clean as ever. He turned round to let me see the name Yorke on the back of his shirt.

A very loud loudspeaker announced the names and numbers of the players – and the whole crowd cheered wildly at Dwight's name. What was interesting though, when he did appear, was that people stood back, in reverence, clapping politely. No one rushed forward or shoved autograph books in his face. Perhaps kids don't have them in Tobago, with few star signatures to capture.

Dwight made a point of going across to a man in a wheelchair and shaking his hand. Then he posed for photos with the referee and linesmen, who seemed to dwarf him. He was in white, playing for Tobago, and wearing number 19 – his Manchester United number. Trinidad were in red.

I positioned myself behind Bertille. He had come out holding the hand of his eight-year-old daughter, Pia, who sat down beside him on the trainers' bench. He cuddled her from time to time, especially when she started growing bored. On his hands and wrists, he had about five sets of gold rings and bracelets, which I hadn't noticed previously. When a space on the bench became vacant, I pushed in beside him. Not much chance of doing that at Old Trafford.

'Well played little boy,' he jumped up and shouted at one of his players.

'Oh gosh,' he shouted, when a mistake was made.

I didn't hear him swear or blaspheme, commonplace on all British benches, yes even Old Trafford, though of course he might have been holding back because of his daughter. The crowd weren't swearing either, or chanting ruderies, though not far behind me I could see and hear some men who had knocked back quite a few beers.

'Don't give your balls away,' one of them shouted at the Tobago team, which had them all holding their sides with laughter.

Dwight should have scored with a header, but the

Trinidad goalie managed to bundle it out, only for another Tobago player to follow up and score. One nil to little Tobago. It didn't last. Trinidad were clearly better, bigger, faster and eventually won 3–1. Dwight stayed on almost to the very end. He looked lively in patches, if not exactly energetic. He got a big cheer when he did come off, at which point many of the female spectators, old as well as young, decided to leave. Something to tell their grandchildren.

It was only when the match was finishing that I realised that Tobago's number 34 was Colvin Hutchinson. All week he'd been one of the people I'd tried to track down. After failing at Villa, he'd last been heard of, so Dwight had told me, working at the airport. But nobody at the airport knew where he was.

I grabbed him after the match and found him friendly and open. I had been led to believe he was basically quiet and introverted and still depressed by what had happened.

He did work at the airport on his return, so he said, thanks to Neil Wilson who had fixed him up with a job. No, not as a baggage handler, but as a clerk. Later, when he had saved up, he went to England again, paying his own fare, and got a job as a semi pro with Andover in the Wessex league. 'I stayed for about five months. It didn't lead to anything and I ran out of money.'

He returned to Tobago, back to his airport job, till a year ago something unexpected happened – Trinidad acquired a professional football league. It's sponsored by Craven A, the cigarette company. Colvin plays for a team called the W Connection, after Jack Warner. While West Indian cricket is doing poorly, football in the Caribbean would seem to be flourishing, in Jamaica, Trinidad and elsewhere.

It means that at the age of 30, Colvin has at long last become a professional footballer. Hence, perhaps, his rather cheerful countenance. He now lives in Trinidad, unmarried, but has three children.

His football pay isn't huge, though he wouldn't tell me exactly how much he earns. The new league has a minimum wage of TT$2,000 (about £200) a month – the same as a labourer earns. A top player might get about TT$8,000.

'You have to negotiate,' he said with a smile. From what he indicated, and others told me, I estimated he was probably getting about £300 a month. That's what Dwight can lose on one game of cards on the team coach.

So what about Dwight's reputed salary?

'Quite fantastic,' he said. 'But I still hope I'll make it.'

Oh really?

'Oh yes, you have to. I think I've got two or three good years left in me. So why not?'

I wished him luck. Well, all footballers need luck. Even Dwight.

I later rang the *Trinidad Guardian*, in Port of Spain, and spoke to its sports editor, Valentino Singh, to check out some details of T and T football and talk about Dwight.

'I first saw Dwight when he was 17 in that vital World Cup game we lost to the USA. At the end he was on his knees, a little boy crying. It was so emotional that match. Everyone who was there will never forget it. But we also remember 1974 when we got robbed by one point. Oh yes, robbed, it was a scandal.'

Back to Dwight. Is it true that people from Tobago have always had it harder than people from Trinidad?

'Oh yes, it is much more diffcult. You have to be outstanding to be noticed. But when you do come through, eyes are focused on you. In a way, his poverty and deprivation helped.'

How?

'If people see you have talent, they try to give you good advice, if they know you are poor with an absentee father. It can work in your favour.'

He thought Colvin was the better player, when they both went off for their trial. 'Colvin was the workhorse in midfield. Dwight had the potential, but at the time, you would have picked Colvin for your team.'

I asked what Trinidadians thought about Dwight's so-called sex scandals.

'Let him who is without sin cast the first stone. No one cares here. Men are the same everywhere. Businessmen, politicians, everyone. They pursue women, go out liming, have a life. It's just that more eyes here are focused on Dwight and Brian Lara than on ordinary people.'

During the last World Cup, in France, he got Dwight to do a column for his paper. 'I rang him each day and talked to him. His comments were very good, more analytical than I expected. He was very good all round. And reliable. He was always where he said he would be, and willing to give me time.'

Lucky you, I thought. Let's hope he's there tomorrow, where and when he said he would be.

41 I found the house where Dwight was staying, La Maison Verte, a large, attractive mainly wooden villa with lawns and gardens and a swimming pool, backing on to the Mount Irvine golf course. I could see a couple of gardeners, gardening away, and a few cars. Unlike at his Cheshire mansion, there was no sign of any security system or metal gates to keep out visitors.

He had said 'Come for brunch about eleven, we'll be able to talk in peace for a few hours, don't worry.'

A woman who looked like a housekeeper let me in, without asking any questions. Yes, Dwight was here, she said, still in bed. That was something. But when I walked through into the main large reception, overlooking the pool and lawns, I discovered I wasn't the only visitor. Half of Tobago was already there.

Gathered round a large table were eight young men, about Dwight's age, playing cards. Had they just arrived or been here all night? There was loud music, a lot of laughing and shouting, slapping backs, banging the table, drinking bottles of Carib beer. One of them was a rasta, with dreadlocks, but the others looked much like Dwight, neat and tidy with close cropped hair. One said hello and it was Garth, his brother. He brought me a Carib, which was kind.

Then I recognised Rama among the card players, and also Sherwin Patrick. If only Dwight had told me they might be here, I could have saved a fortune in taxis having spent the last five days trekking all over the island trying to track them down. I suppose I had helped the economy.

Outside, on the lawns, in a summer house, another party seemed to be going on, but much quieter. They were mostly older men, sipping drinks, looking pensive. Perhaps not a party. More like a queue. Oh no. They were probably waiting to see Dwight. Had been for ages, by their pensive, resigned faces.

One of the young men inside, watching the card players, said hi, how's it going. He looked very couth and polished. Turned out to be Kona Hislop, brother of Shaka, the ex-Newcastle and now West Ham goalkeeper. Kona lives in Newcastle, doing nothing very much. He'd come out from England with Dwight on the plane for a holiday. Like Shaka, he was born in London, where their father was studying law. They all then returned to Trinidad. Their father, now retired, became a successful lawyer.

I recognised one of the older men outside as Clint, another of Dwight's brothers. Not that he is old, at 38, just older than the ones playing cards. He was the one who became a professional cricketer, now a security guard. I asked which teams he'd played for in England. Todmorden, in the Lancashire League, then one in County Durham.

Altogether, he'd had four years in England. I said it must be very different, being back.

'Yes, more relaxed. There's too much rushing in the developed world. We also don't push our noses into areas we don't know about, not till we know what the reaction might be. It's two different worlds. Things you might think OK, we think offensive. We think people are entitled to a private life. Over there, celebrities get stalked. We might be watching them, but we keep our distance ...'

Very true, but was he also getting at me? Then to my surprise, I realised that sitting next to him, in baseball cap, drinking a beer, was Fulton. I had imagined he might be persona non grata with the sons of the Yorke family, yet here he was.

I said hello, re-introduced myself, and this time, realising that I must be Dwight's friend, sort of, he agreed to talk.

That was when he took me through his life, blow by blow, date by date, all his various jobs. He made me write down names, and read back the spellings of firms he had worked with many years ago.

What I most wanted to hear about was his relationship with his family. Whether or not he was an absentee father, as many people in Tobago believe.

'No. I always lived at home,' he said, staring me straight in the eye, as if daring me to disprove it.

'It's only in the last year I don't sleep there, from April 1998. Until then, that was my home.'

I asked if all the children were his. 'You've seen them. What do you think? Don't they look like me?'

I said, well, Clint had his build, being tall, and Verlaine is quite big, but the other three brothers I'd seen are smaller.

'Yes, but they all look like me.'

So they are yours?

'Yes, all mine. I have only one kid outside my marriage.'

And did you always help financially?

'Of course I did. When I could, when I had money.'

So what made you leave last year?

'Certain developments arose, certain tings happened, which I don't want to get into. I don't want to degrade Dwight.

'Dwight never showed me no different. We still talk. If anyting happened between me and his mother, I tell him the truth. Sometimes he did say "Dad, don't be stupid". But I'm not going into that. I'm not washing my dirty linen in public.'

Of course not, I said. I had to ask to establish the basic facts, so I don't get anything wrong. During Dwight's career, most local people seemed to assume his father was not always around, so people did their best to help, to compensate.

He thought about this for some time, then spoke slowly, at dictation speed.

'All I want you to say is that Dwight's father is an honest and straightforward man.'

Then he added, almost as an afterthought. 'And I'm a man who done nothing that all men don't do ...'

I thanked him for his help. Dwight had now got up and had appeared, chatting inside to some of his chums, but looking a bit stressed and moody. He came outside, said hi. His shirt was off and I could see clearly the burn mark on his back, caused by the road accident. It was very large. And it did look like a map of Tobago.

He asked if I was OK, if I wanted another beer, wanted something to eat. He was eating in a minute and would fetch me something. But in the meantime he just had a couple of people to speak to.

He sat down with one of the older men at a table. They appeared to be discussing money. Then with another man about some meeting. At last it was my turn, though other people still came across to chat or ask him things.

I said he looked a bit fed up. He said yeah, it was because

of all these people here. Some hadn't been invited, they'd just walked in, and were now drinking his drink, abusing his hospitality.

He then stood up and gave a loud groan. Through the open doors of the reception room he had seen that the Channel Four television crew had walked in uninvited.

'That's what happens when I have open house. People take liberties. It's so impolite. It really pisses me off.'

It was the first time, in many conversations, I had heard Dwight swear. Though pretty mild swearing, for a foot-baller.

'I don't know what's going on. I don't know who half these people are.'

I knew that Rama and Sherwin were his old friends, but if some of the others weren't, why not just chuck them out?

'I don't like doing that. I don't like causing scenes, effing and blinding. That's not me. I don't like confrontations.'

Because you want to remain popular?

'I don't know about that,' he said, managing a wry smile. 'OK, that's probably it.'

So what are you going to do about it?

'I've told my friends that they must not let them in. Try to ease them out. Otherwise, they won't be invited back.'

So, getting others to do your dirty work? In which case I completely understood. I have gone through life myself trying to be popular, avoiding arguments with people. Sometimes it can be so exhausting, being nice. He smiled.

Having got clear on this occasion what was pissing him off, which often he won't reveal, trying to be doubly a nice person, but only getting himself in contortions, I asked about his hols. His so-called hols. Being back in Tobago.

'I do like it here. I love my country, but I never seem to have time to properly relax when I'm here. But I will. I plan to explore more, when I've time. I still haven't been to places like Castara or Englishman's Bay which all visitors rave about. I suppose I must have been in most of the villages, as a boy, going to play football matches, but I don't remember any of them. I did go to Pigeon Point, sneaking in without paying.

'But the more I do come back, the more I realise how beautiful my country is. I took it for granted, when I lived here. Now I do want to see it all. The people are so nice, so laid back. I like their attitude. Except when some are taking liberties ...'

He stood up again, spotting someone he didn't know, who had wandered in.

After a decade in England, he must though get irritated by various little things about Tobago, services not working, people not being exactly punctual.

'When I moved into this house, the phone wasn't working, which made me mad. You know how I live on the phone. So I rang up the phone people to complain and they weren't interested, said it would take weeks. But when I gave my name, their attitude changed at once. They were round to mend it in minutes. It shouldn't be like that.'

You mean officials shouldn't want to keep in with the famous?

'They should be helpful and efficient with all customers, whoever they are. That's what I mean.

'But once I am here, well, I soon get to adjust to the local pace of life.'

I told him about the people from his past I'd been talking to all week. How some were not just impressed by his football skills but his language skills. Had he worked on that, gone to lessons?

'No, but in those early years, I wasn't just sitting around watching television at Sheila's, as she might have thought. I used to read everything I could find. English newspapers, paperbacks, anything to improve my English skills. I'd look up words I didn't know.

'I still do that. For example when there was some sex story about me in a tabloid which had the word "romp" in a headline.'

I thought you didn't read newspapers? So you told me. It is true I'd never seen a newspaper in his house.

'I don't get any delivered. Someone must have given it to me. Anyway, I wanted to look up the word "romp". They'd made it look as if I'd slept with this girl, which wasn't true, so I wanted to know its correct meaning. I hadn't heard the word before. So I looked it up. It turns out fairly harmless. It just means "fun", really ...'

Yes, but when they say 'sex romps', every reader knows what that means, nudge nudge.

'I realise that. They are so clever, these English tabloids. Makes it very hard to sue them.'

I also mentioned that several of these older friends felt he should be contributing more to his country. He gave a big sigh.

'I get this all the time. People wanting me to open things, go to functions, help in some way. But my schedule doesn't allow me to do all the things I'm asked.

'I have tried to help, when I can. I've assisted Signal Hill, one of my old schools. When I do a deal with a sponsor, I try to get them to donate money or equipment, as part of the deal.

'The trouble is you don't always know which people or charities are honest and deserving. It's very hard. And out here, there's only one of me. Everyone is after me, all the time, for money.

'I have my own family to think of first – my mother, brothers and sisters. Then my handful of real old friends. They come first, not people who alleged they helped me. It gets ridiculous at times, people turning up to take credit for what I've done. I haven't got enough money anyway, just to throw it away.

'But yeah, I will at some stage do something. I don't know what. But I do want to put something back into the island. The opportunity will arise.'

As he was speaking, one of the older men came over and started to tell him about his wife being ill. Could Dwight

just pop into his house some time? Dwight knew where it
was. She was lying in bed, ill, but seeing Dwight would
cheer her up. Dwight said he'd try, but his schedule was
very busy.

'Now for me,' continued the man. 'I'm three months
behind with the rent. I need TT$900, at once.'

Dwight took a bundle of blue TT$100 notes from his
pocket and handed some over. He then went to where his
father was still sitting and slipped him some money as well.

When he came back, he said he was looking at properties
in Tobago where he could stay in the future, instead of using
a hotel or renting. What about this house, I said. Seems
pretty good. He was considering that. The asking price was
US$1.1 million. Sounded reasonable, I said. And the rental
income would be good, if he wanted to let it when he wasn't
here. He was thinking about that.

I contacted the agent later and found that the rate was
US$500 a day in the high season, US$385 in the low season.
Tobago is currently expanding as a holiday island, with
many very exclusive houses and up market hotels being
built. I like to think that young Dwight would therefore be
making a sensible investment.

He then had to go to a meeting in Scarborough with some
people to discuss the new stadium being built, the one
which might have his name on it.

I walked with him back through the house. His friends
were still playing cards, drinking and laughing. He slapped
a few backs, exchanged a few laughs, the ever popular
Dwight.

I said it was interesting that he'd kept all these friends
from his past, ones he'd been to school with, or older people
from his neighbourhood, rather than acquiring new
people from the business or entrepreneur class, whom he
must since have met along the way. They did exist, at least
in Trinidad.

'It is important for me to keep my old friends. And it's

important for me that they think I haven't changed. Some people think I have changed, that I'm now a big superstar. I don't think so. But I like to feel in their eyes I'm still the same person I always was. That matters to me.'

We arranged to meet again in England, if I had any other questions for him. Loads, I said. Though whether I would get loads of time, or loads of answers ...

Grace Yorke, Dwight's mother on her porch at home in Tobago. HUNTER DAVIES

Dwight Yorke's street. HUNTER DAVIES

Grace Yorke's home in 1999, where Dwight was born. HUNTER DAVIES

Clint Yorke, Dwight's brother who was a professional cricketer and is now a security guard. HUNTER DAVIES

Garth Yorke, another of Dwight's brothers is a Rodent operative and lives at home. HUNTER DAVIES

Dwight's primary school, Bon Accord Government School. HUNTER DAVIES

Fulton Yorke, Dwight's father.
HUNTER DAVIES

Kenny Crooks, Dwight's teacher at Bon Accord who looked after sport.
HUNTER DAVIES

Orville London, teacher at Signal Hill Comprehensive School. He later became Principal and is now Sports Editor of *Tobago News*. HUNTER DAVIES

Sherwin Patrick, goalie for the school football team, with whom Dwight went to live aged 14. He is now a barber. HUNTER DAVIES

Rama, Dwight Yorke's best friend as a boy. HUNTER DAVIES

Neil Wilson, the businessman who became Dwight's 'manager'. HUNTER DAVIES

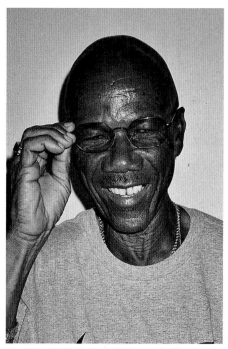

Bertille St Clair, Dwight's coach from the age of eight. HUNTER DAVIES

Colvin Hutchinson who went with Dwight for the trial at Aston Villa. He never made it. HUNTER DAVIES

Deborah Moore-Miggins, the lawyer who negotiated Dwight's contract with Aston Villa. She is the sister of Wendell Moore, Yorke's idol as a boy, and Dwight Moore, the boy Dwight was named after. HUNTER DAVIES

Shaw Park, Tobago where Dwight first played football. HUNTER DAVIES

The local crowd, many of them girls, who came to see Dwight play in Tobago. HUNTER DAVIES

Dwight Yorke, number 19, with the referee and his assistants, before playing in a friendly for Tobago against Trinidad at Shaw Park, Tobago, June 1999. HUNTER DAVIES

(Above) Hunter Davies in Dwight's rented house on Tobago, in 1999. HUNTER DAVIES

(Right) Sheila and Bryn. Sheila was Dwight's first landlady – she was known as 'Mums'. HUNTER DAVIES

Sheila and Bryn's cottage at Shustoke. Dwight's first home in the UK. HUNTER DAVIES

(Above) Dwight's home in Cheshire.
HUNTER DAVIES

(Left) Dwight Yorke at home with some of his trophies.
HUNTER DAVIES

Part 5
ENGLAND

42 Meanwhile, back in a typical English country cottage, in a typical English village, Sheila is pasting in the latest on D. Yorke in her scrapbook. From his arrival at her house in 1990, she has cut out references to him in the *Mirror* and the *Sun*, the two dailies she normally gets, plus the local Birmingham papers. There are now six albums, carefully pasted, beautifully preserved.

I was allowed to look through them, as my hands were clean at the time, and they were jolly interesting, but alas a bit limited for my purposes. They were mainly either match reports or news stories but rarely any decent length interviews or biographical stuff or broadsheet coverage. She had also omitted to write in the date and name of the newspaper on each cutting, so some were hard to place. But, still, a great piece of work, nay devotion. No mother could have been more loyal. But what is she keeping them for?

'For his future wife, of course,' said Sheila. 'And his children. I want them to be able to read what their father did.'

Does that, er, include his romps?

'Oh no. Didn't you notice I haven't cut out any of the scandal stories. None of that kiss-and-tell rubbish. I wouldn't want his future wife to see that sort of crap, would I?

'Oh I do hope he will get married. He'll make a lovely husband and a perfect father. I just worry that the more he lives on his own, the more he gets used to his own space. He might not want to share it. But I think he will ...'

Like almost everyone who has been part of Dwight's life, here and in Tobago, Sheila says she was always sure he would make it.

'I knew he had talent. Everyone said so. My only worry was would he be physically aggressive enough on the pitch. He's just too nice a person to be aggressive, too polite. I don't think I've ever seen him lose his temper. Get depressed, yes, but not angry. You just have to see him on television in a match. Other players are effing and blinding at the referee, all scowls when they get told off, or a decision goes against them. Dwight just walks away smiling.'

What did Andy Comyn predict? And what does he think now about Dwight? Andy was Dwight's room mate at Sheila's, back in ancient times, the graduate footballer who was very helpful. He got ahead of Dwight, in the race to make a first team debut.

On 24 October 1990, he was in the first team against Inter Milan in the UEFA Cup which they won 2–0. In the return match, Paul McGrath, whom Andy had replaced, had recovered from injury and was in the team. Villa lost 3–0 and so went out.

In the Villa programme for 10 November 1990, there is a whole page devoted to Andy. 'Andy Comyn has to pinch himself to make sure that everything that has happened to him is true. From non-league Alvechurch to facing the mighty Inter Milan via Wembley in just over 12 months is the breakneck progress made by Comyn. But no one can dispute that Comyn has staked a worthy claim for a regular first team spot.'

Alas, after that, Andy did not do so well. As happened with several other Villa players, the promotion of Graham Taylor to the England job did not help his career.

'Graham had signed me, so naturally I had a soft spot for him. Still have. When Ron Atkinson came, he had more pulling power and was given more money to spend. We were on a pre-season tour to Hanover in 1991 when he drew me aside and said that Arthur Cox of Derby was interested in me. The clubs had agreed a fee. Now it was up to me. He made it clear that Paul McGrath would be first choice to start the season. I was just one of five others next in line. It was clear I wasn't going to get many starts. So I went to Derby. I was disappointed to leave. Yeah, I suppose I could have stayed and fought for my place, but it seemed the obvious and sensible thing to do.'

In his first season with Derby, Andy played every game. Next season, he had around 30 games, but by then some new players had been signed and his position was no longer secure. He moved down a division to Plymouth, from 1993–96, then had a short spell with West Brom, before deciding to call it a day.

He was only 28, around Dwight's age today, but felt he would not progress any further, that it was time to get into another career. Unlike Dwight, and the vast majority of players, he did have his degree behind him.

'I got offered a chance to play non-league for Hednesford Town – and the manager turned out to have an accountancy firm in Birmingham. I've now been working for that firm for two years. I'm half way through my exams to be a qualified accountant. I don't get anything like the money in football, but eventually I should have a decent career.'

Andy, now aged 32, is married to Rebecca who runs her own nursery school. They have two children, Oliver aged four who supports Arsenal and Libby aged three.

'In some ways yes, I am disappointed my football career didn't quite work out. It was an up and down career, but I loved every moment of it. I wish I'd appreciated it more at the time. I mean playing against Inter Milan, I was hardly aware of what was happening. It came so quickly.'

Dwight's career, so far, has had no serious, long-term dips, going ever upwards. Was his success a surprise?

'I have to admit that I did not expect Dwight would be

where he is now. He had the skill, that was clear, and the desire to improve, but I thought he was naïve and over-confident. You need to be confident, but that incident when he thought he would beat everyone on the Long Run, that stuck in my mind. It seemed pure over-confidence.

'Then there was our weather. He hated the mud. It just didn't suit him. I thought he wouldn't be strong enough to survive. And in those early years, he wasn't much of a team player. He would beat players instead of passing.'

So what did it? 'Dedication, for a start. With all success-ful players, there is an inner desire. They constantly see their goal to play at the highest level. They are willing to learn, to change, to do anything to achieve it. That's what Dwight's done.

'I didn't see it at the time, but I did later. You don't always see these things, which is why you can never tell who will make it. Often they don't quite cotton on when they're young. It hits them later.

'With coming from the West Indies, that seemed it could be a problem, adapting to our culture. Then you never know if someone who is good in the reserves will keep his confi-dence in the first team. It can all go, at that stage.

'I still worried about him when he went to Manchester United. They have a history of forwards who didn't make it. Remember Peter Davenport, Alan Brazil. Their confidence went when they got there. Dwight did surprise me, and many others.

'I can't see him losing that desire now, even at the top. He must have enough money not to play again, but he's like David Beckham. You can't stop that desire.

'Dwight loves the crowd, loves being appreciated. That's another reason why he'll go on, for as long as he can.

'I met him at a club in Birmingham, not long after he'd joined Manchester United. It was the time when one of those scandal stories had appeared, the one with the dodgy video at Mark Bosnich's. I talked to him about it and he seemed resigned to it. "That's the price you pay for being in the public eye."

'I'm not saying he likes that sort of publicity. But he was taking it in his stride, being mature about it.'

Andy was of course delighted to be recognised by Dwight on the last occasion their paths crossed – at Bisham Abbey, just before the 1999 Cup Final at Wembley.

What were you doing there, Andy?

'Oh I happened to be in a training session for the England Non-League semi-professional team. It was nice when Dwight said, "Hi Jeeves, how's it going?" No one has called me that since I left Villa …'

One of the real stars at Villa when Dwight and Andy were trying to break through, acclaimed by all and later awarded with England caps, was Tony Daley. It was at his mother's house that Dwight stayed for a while and was not very happy. Mrs Daley is still in the same house – but had recently been very ill and was in hospital, recovering.

As for Tony, he remained at Villa and was in the 1994 Coca-Cola Cup Final team, the one which Dwight didn't make.

'I remember talking to him about being dropped. Not beforehand. Afterwards. Before a match, you don't care about other players and their problems. You are only concerned with yourself, getting focused. He was devastated by what happened and felt he'd had enough. I told him he would have other opportunities. I think it probably did make him stronger for the future.'

Tony left Villa not long afterwards, after 230 first team games and 36 goals. He was transferred to Wolves for £1.5 million and was there four seasons. But alas, out of those four seasons, only one was any good.

'I lost three years of my life through injury. The first rupture kept me out for 18 months. When I came back, it still wasn't right and I was told I could never play again, even though I was only 28. I did get back from that, once again. But I was in and out of the team, going nowhere.'

In 1998 he moved to Watford, where the manager was Graham Taylor, his old manager from Villa. He rarely made the first team and in the summer of 1999, they decided not to renew his contract.

When I spoke to him, he had just got off a plane from China where he had been for a trial with a Chinese club. 'The money was good, but not the conditions. I didn't fancy it, so I'm not taking it.'

He was still living in digs in Watford, while his wife and two children were at home in Birmingham, wondering what to do next, or if at the age of 32, that was the end.

'I don't regret anything in my own career. I am proud of my seven England caps and my League Cup Final medal. I don't want to continue in football as a coach or manager. I don't think I can take the pressures. I'd like to be on the fitness side, a personal fitness trainer perhaps, something like that.'

Did he feel at all envious of Dwight, a mere boy when he had been Villa's big star, who has been lucky enough, so far, to escape any career threatening injuries?

'I feel nothing but admiration for Dwight. He's done brilliant. To be honest, I didn't know if he'd be able to adapt to British life, with his laid-back, West Indian attitudes. I thought with his talent, he'd make a good living as a professional, but not be the world-class player he is now. Oh yes. Even in China, people who follow football, they all know his name.

'I think he will get even better. There is more to come. Who knows what he will achieve in the end.'

One person still at Villa from Dwight's generation is Ugo Ehiogu. Like Tony, he didn't see Dwight as a world-class player, not at 17.

'I thought he might make the first team and get 20 games, but that was about all. It was only when I played with him that I saw his skills and I thought, "Blimey, he could be special."

'By the time he left Villa for Manchester United, we all knew his quality. People were envious when he left, but not jealous. We were pleased for him. Some pundits thought he might struggle at Manchester United, but I didn't. We knew his quality. And at Manchester United he would get more chances than he'd had at Villa.

'He's had to change a bit at Manchester United, but he learns quickly. You're in a goldfish bowl, up there. You have to learn to be a bit more unapproachable. Because everyone is after you.'

As for the managers who looked after him at Villa, they all maintain they always knew how good he was.

'When he was transferred to Manchester United,' says Ron Atkinson, 'some people at Manchester United asked me about him. I said it wouldn't be Sheringham and Cole he would help most, or any other of the forwards, but the midfield. They'll be very grateful for him, for coming back and helping, holding up the ball.

'No, I'm not surprised he settled in so well. I think he arrived high on adrenalin – and it never left him.

'He's now got a superb collection of players around him, so I think he'll get even better. I see him in midfield, eventually, not as a striker. Oh yes, there's more in him yet ...'

Dear Ron himself doesn't appear to have a lot more in him, not as a manager. After a brief spell at Nottingham Forest, he officially retired in the summer of 1999, to count his money, his suits, probably his bottles of champagne, and to delight us with his television commentaries.

Graham Taylor's management career appeared to have nosedived at one stage, after being treated as a turnip during his time as England manager. He had one uneventful season at Wolves, then returned to Watford where once again he performed miracles, hauling them through the divisions to the Premier League in the 1999–2000 season.

'I'm not at all surprised Dwight has done so well,' says Graham. 'I could tell it at 17, when we first saw him. He could handle anything. He had come 10,000 miles from a different culture, but he adapted at once. I have known grown men, mature players, move 100 miles, and be unable to cope with the culture shock.

'I signed David Platt and Paul McGrath, both excellent players, but with Dwight, I had spotted him myself, backed my judgement when he was unknown, untrained. I did the same with John Barnes. I found him. No, I tell a lie. A supporter at Watford tipped me off. But he was my discovery. So was Dwight. I am more proud of discovering them than almost anything I've done in football.

'I knew Dwight would cope at Manchester United. It wouldn't defeat him. He rang me before the Bayern match in Barcelona. I wasn't in but he left an answerphone message. When I came in, to watch the match, I played back the message and found it was Dwight, ringing to thank me for what I had done for his career, and hoping I would be proud of him tonight.

'I shouted to Rita, come and listen to this. I played her the message as well. It was incredible. I was almost in tears, listening to it. It made up for many things that have happened to me in life, not just in football, but life generally. No, you don't get many like Dwight ...'

John Gregory, after Dwight left so acrimoniously, had the satisfaction of seeing Villa shoot to the top of the table. They stayed there for most of the first half of the season, though fell away towards the end, finishing up seventh, but made a profit of £20 million in the season.

'Yes, we did do very well when he went. We do have some very talented players here and I think they wanted to prove they were not just a one-man team. They thought, "Yeah,

Dwight's a great player, but so are we, we'll show the fans."
It made them very determined.

'I expected Dwight to do well at Manchester United. He
has very high standards. He's a tough, hard cookie, which
people don't quite realise. Then he's had to be, arriving here
with nothing. He's put in the hard work, worked his socks off.
That's what I mean by hard. He's also nice with it. No disrespect to Tobago, but it's a shame he's not from some big
European country, then he would have been seen on a World
Cup stage.

'He was certainly worth £12 million – especially when
you think that Vieri has been sold for £31 million …

'I don't consider we fell out. I was just upset that he wanted
to go. I did ring him before the match in Barcelona. I said this
is it, this is what you went for, and wished him luck.'

There is no doubt about Dwight's success and total acceptance at Manchester United. The fears expressed by some
people at the time of his signing – that the fee was too
much, that he was untested at the highest level, or might
disappear – have all been forgotten.

Alex Ferguson has admitted that he had tried to sign
other forwards around that time, but then he often has, over
the years, and failed, for one reason or other. He didn't get
Shearer, John Barnes, Brian Laudrup, Gascoigne when he
wanted them. More recently there was interest in
Batistuta, Salas and Kluivert. Dwight was a bit of a
surprise to many, in the same way that Cantona was a
surprise – but the effects have been similar.

'I'll tell you what he does for us,' so Ferguson has said. 'He
does what Cantona did. He scores important goals.
Whatever the game, you think, "Yorkie will get us one." '

But even he was surprised by how quickly he settled,
knowing how players in the past have frozen, especially pre-
1993, before the modern Manchester United had started to
win things.

'Sometimes the desire to win things can be too strong. A lot of players, particularly strikers, came to the club and couldn't handle the pressures. But after we won the Championship in 1993, I think players who have arrived at the club since have been able to settle more easily. Dwight Yorke is a prime example.'

In his autobiography, Sir Alex appears quite critical of Dwight's performance in that final European match against Bayern. 'I thought Dwight Yorke, who may be as talented a front player as there is in the game today, looked more nervous than I had ever previously seen him. It did not help, of course, that he was opposed by a brilliant marker.'

However, elsewhere he has nothing but praise. 'From the moment he joined us, Dwight had justified my conviction that he was a front player with a remarkable range of exceptional abilities. He is effortlessly neat on the ball, can beat opponents with swift dribbles or imaginative passes and is an excellent finisher. He has the heart and bodily strength to thrive in tough company and his joyous appetite for the game shines through the smile which is nearly always on his face.'

In the dressing room, according to Gary Neville, Dwight from the beginning added as much off the field as on it. 'He seemed to fit in almost straight away with the lads.

'I don't think I've ever come across anyone with his character. He's so completely relaxed. There's no edge to him, no tensions. He likes everybody and everybody likes him. He obviously thinks life is too short to hate people.

'I am quite tense, myself, but even when he'd just been here a few weeks, he was putting his arm round my shoulder saying "what's happening – just relax". I'm always waiting for things to happen. I find it hard to relax.

'We've never been what you'd call a quiet dressing room at Manchester United, but if it's getting a bit quieter than normal, like before a really big game, Dwight will break it up. He's probably become the loudest, playing games and stuff – but that's because he's the happiest. He's had a good effect on us all. He's been magnificent.'

So magnificent he wasn't picked for the FA Cup Final?

'Yes, I saw the disappointment in his face. He was trying not to let it show, but I saw. But that was the Gaffer's decision. He has drummed it into us that we're in a squad. You have to expect not to play sometimes.

'I'm sure Dwight does suffer the same little worries and stresses we all have. But unlike most of us, he hides those problems.

'I remember seeing him upset because his house had been photographed and was in the newspapers. At Manchester United, you get used to that sort of thing. It was new to him, that sort of attention.

'We have of course given him some stick in the dressing room every time he's in the *News of the World*. You expect that as well.

'Looking back to his arrival, what no one expected was he'd score 29 goals and we'd win the Treble. That would have been in the realm of dreams ...'

Tony Stephens is still Dwight's agent, though in the last year his own firm has been bought by an American firm, Marquee, making him a nice capital sum. It has been merged with another, similar British agency which handles footballers, run by Jon Holmes in Nottingham. Together their portfolio of star footballers includes Shearer, Beckham, Owen, Dion Dublin, Gary Lineker, Graeme Le Saux, Garry McAllister and Emile Heskey.

They are both now directors of Marquee UK. Holmes is the more outgoing and sociable, likes a drink or two. Tony is quiet, discreet, dark suited, abstemious, keeps a low profile. You never see him quoted in the papers. They even have different philosophies on handling players.

'I remember discussing star players with Jon when we joined forces. He believes you should keep them apart – so that each thinks you are exclusively looking after them, giving them your whole attention. I take the opposite view. I like my clients to meet and know each other, because wisdom can then trickle down the generations.

'I was at Alan Shearer's house a few years ago, and Michael Owen's father rang me. Michael had been playing for England Youth, as captain, and had got a red card and been sent off. He was absolutely devastated, so his father rang for my advice. I talked to him for a bit, then Alan, sitting in the room, who'd heard what had happened, said give me the phone. He talked directly to Michael's father, telling him how to handle it, what to tell Michael. Now I think that was marvellous – getting first-hand advice from the England captain, when you're only a teenager. That's why I never keep my clients apart.'

Right, back to Dwight, star of this show. How do you think he has done, so far?

'I had no worries about Dwight doing well at Manchester United,' says Tony, 'but he settled even quicker and better than I expected. He's an outgoing personality, so that helps. He walked into the Theatre of Dreams – and immediately became one of the star cast.

'Everything you do in life is an apprenticeship for what you are going to do next. That disappointment at Villa when he didn't make the Coca-Cola final team prepared him for Manchester United. When that chance came, he made the most of it.

'He has matured enormously over the years. I was for him buying his first house, not just as a sound investment but as part of the maturing process, part of his growing up.

'I first noticed a change at the end of the 1994 season. He arranged for me and my wife and secretary to have dinner with him. He'd booked a Chinese restaurant in Sutton Coldfield, a very nice one. He personally went into the kitchen to see the chef and discuss the menu. He wouldn't let us choose anything. He did it all. Then at the end of the meal, he gave my wife and secretary a silk scarf each and I got a bottle of vintage port.

'Until that time, he was the sort of typical young player, who has everything done for them, always has done, since he joined his club as a youth player. He expects that to go on.

'But there comes a point with the really intelligent, sensible, organised ones who decide they have to do things for themselves, to find out how things work, then organise their own life.

'So I saw that dinner he'd organised as the point of change for Dwight. He has been his own man, ever since. He's been able to organise his life far better than I think anyone ever expected, yet still appearing casual and laid back.

'He's still a lovely lad. He's consistent, loyal and has a sense of fun. Both my daughters, aged 20 and 18, love him, and they have grown up with seeing famous footballers around the house. They adore him. Everyone does.

'I would love him to meet Miss Right. He will make a wonderful husband and great father. It is true that in the past he was only meeting model girl sort of girls. I think all the kiss-and-tell stories, with all their inaccuracies, have made him more careful. I think he would like to be married – but of course sometimes you can look too hard. I think he is keen to be married. It just hasn't happened yet.

'He is being offered far more commercial work, now that he is at Manchester United. But with Dwight, football comes first, second and third. He doesn't do half of what he could do.

'With all my players, I never do one-offs. By that I mean opening a bingo hall or a new Tesco. I am only interested in medium- to long-term commitments, which will help the image of my client.

'I now don't think he will ever play abroad, as I once did. David Platt was very keen because he wanted that experience, of being in a new country, savouring a new culture. Dwight has done that – by coming here.

'He's now with the world's biggest club, so why should he want to move? Compared with ten years ago, the big money and opportunities are here. There is no need to go to Italy to feel you're playing at the top.

'I don't know what he will do after his career is over. He'll end up wealthy, but he will have to protect his wealth, not put it at risk. He has professional help with that.

'We haven't really discussed it. He wants to stay playing as long as possible, as he loves it so much.

'He has a media-attractive personality and though he hasn't done much, I'm sure he could do well on television. We'll see. With all my clients, I like to think I can help with the rest of their life, not just their football life.'

43 Dwight was at home looking forward to a new season that had just begun. But what could a new season bring that the old season didn't bring? As the Queen so sagely observed to Sir Alex, the Treble will not be done again.

Personally, I wouldn't be too sure. We thought doing the Double was a minor miracle, or at least extremely rare, when Spurs did it in 1961, now it happens quite regularly. Our three or four top teams have increasingly the best players and most resources, which should make them more likely to leave clear water between themselves and the pack behind, panting in the distance. I would certainly not bet on England winning the World Cup again, not in my lifetime, or the life of anyone living, but I would not be at all surprised if Manchester United did the Treble again in the next decade.

All the same, it must have been hard personally for those players who did it in 1998–99, which appeared to be a miraculous, one-off season, to set out of their personal stalls for the season ahead.

'At the beginning of every season,' said Dwight, 'I have always written in my diary what I hope to achieve in the year ahead. At Villa in the early years it was just to get in the first team. Then to be a regular.

'When I joined Manchester United, all I wrote down was that my aim was to be top scorer and to win something. I never imagined we would win THREE things.

'So it was a problem, knowing what to write for this year. I have written down how many goals I'd like to get, but I'm not telling you. My main ambition is still the same – to remain as a regular in the team. At a place like Manchester United, you know there will be new people every season, so you have to fight for your place.

'I am still ambitious. I still see things happening in my head, as I always have done. That hasn't changed now I'm 27.'

Looking back, at your very long life, and at all the people who helped and didn't help, the chances which arrived, such as Villa coming along when they did, how would you evaluate the factors that have contributed to where you are today, and what you have become?

OK, I'll start again. What proportion do you put down to natural talent, to determination and ambition, to luck?

Dwight was of course good at sums at school, so he quite liked thinking in percentages. At first, he gave natural talent the largest percentage by far, then he took it back. He hadn't given luck a big enough share. After several more attempts, rearranging the figures, he decided that 40 per cent had been talent, 40 per cent determination and ambition and 20 per cent was luck.

'In my position, coming from where I came from, luck did play a vital part.'

I talked about Beckham, not his lovely wedding, where Dwight was a well-dressed guest, but how he, Becks, had been born with a silver spoon, comparatively speaking, in the right place, right time, with the right sort of totally supportive family.

'Yeah, but in the end, it's always up to you. It's what you do with your chances. The situation you start from doesn't really matter. It's what's in you that counts. Becks has always worked hard, appreciated what he had to do to succeed. And he did it. Still does it.

'Life was tough for me, but I always thought something would turn up. It would work out, so I was never pessimistic, never thought the world was against me. I just knew I'd do it.'

One of the symbols of his success, apart from the big house, is his cars. Surely for a sensible bloke, not otherwise silly with his money, it's, well, a bit flash, having such expensive cars?

'No, I don't think it's flash. I've always been interested in cars. I always promised myself I'd have a good one. It's something I enjoy. I've worked hard to be able to afford them. It pleases me to have them. I don't live my life to please other people.'

True, but is it necessary to have three, when there's only one of you in this household and you can only drive one at a time?

'But I use all three. It depends on my mood. If it's sunny, or I'm going somewhere exciting, I'll drive my Ferrari. If it's a business meeting, or I'm going out for a meal, I might use the Mercedes. If it's grey, bad weather and wet, I'll use the Range Rover. It all depends how I feel. So I enjoy them all. Yes, I'm a single man, but that also means I have no other responsibilities, have I ...'

Not so far. Though in the meantime, the rest of the world is trying to get him married. His mother and Sheila and Tony all hope or expect him to settle down soon with a partner. What's the problem?

'I have dated some girls who wanted to get closer, but I'm not prepared, not at the moment.'

I had observed that he was quite settled in his bachelor life, seemed happy enough with his own company, making a meal for himself, eating by himself, sleeping in his big house by himself. Well, mostly. One does get used to such a state, and become irritated when other people exert pressures. I had been with him in Birmingham, a few months earlier, when he was moaning about some arrangements for Mark Bosnich's wedding. He was having to go to a rehearsal, saying that was just like women, trying to tie you down to arrangements.

The more his present life goes on, the harder it will be to change it. If of course he ever does want to change it.

'Outside football, I still get most fun from just sitting around playing cards with my friends. But yeah, there are times when I'd like to share the good moments with someone else ...'

And presumably the bad moments as well, when he gets into a mood. Wives or regular partners do have their uses. Groupies can't quite fill that function.

'I don't call them groupies,' he said. 'Just girls. Yes, some do follow me around, but I keep out of the way of them.

'The thing about the girls is that I have done as I have always done. As I did at Villa. There's nothing new. It just gets into the papers now. Sometimes the stories are three or four years old, girls I used to know a long time ago.

'I like to think I have been honest with every girl I've been with. They know the score from day one. They know it's a bit of fun together. And I have never abused any of them, or taken unfair advantage.

'I do hope someone will come along. I do aim to be settled one day and have a family. But I'm not prepared to take second best. I want to reach the heights with a wife, just as I did in football. That takes time – and discipline.'

So what about the future, inside and outside football?

'I have no intention or plans to go anywhere else except Manchester United. But you never know, things change in football. I know I will leave one day. Three years from now, I might decide I need a new challenge. But if I do go anywhere, it will be a let-down, a come-down, after Manchester United. There's no better team or bigger club.'

And the future personally? Would he like to stay in football, as a coach or manager? He made a face, not to dismiss it, just to show he wasn't keen. But then few players at the age of 27 envisage themselves as a manager, seeing too clearly all the pressures, compared with actually playing. Later, when their careers are about to end for good, they often change their mind.

'When I finish, I might get into some business. I don't know what. I can't take on the idea of a business or investments, not at present. I have an accountant and lawyer, they look after all the day-to-day things. I own nothing apart from this house, and maybe if I get one in Tobago. That's all. I couldn't take on an outside venture, not when I'm still playing. There are enough pressures already.

'But when I retire, I might get something. A sports bar perhaps. I wouldn't work there. Just as an investment.

'What I'm thinking of is living six months in Tobago and six months here in England. That would suit me, be my ideal. I shouldn't have to work again, not for money.'

Sounds fun, splitting one's life in two. I do much the same, dividing the year equally between London and Lakeland. I like to think it's like living twice. Though a Caribbean island thrown in might be even nicer.

'Yeah, I'm looking forward to it. It'll be easier, now I have my passport.'

Your what?

'I've now got my British passport.'

Dwighty baby, you're going to be hammered back in Trinidad and Tobago when they hear this. Some will think you're wanting to play for England, which you can't, having already played for T and T.

'That's not the reason of course. It's just that all these

years it's been such a hassle every time I travel anywhere, having to go through different passport places from the other players. Then there's the problem of work permits and stuff. I got so fed up with all that every year. I did ask at Villa, if they could help me get a British passport. After all, I have been resident here all these years. But nothing happened.

'When I mentioned it at Manchester United, they immediately got on to it. Now it's sorted out. It will help so much in the years to come.

'Obviously I don't look upon myself as British. I'm still a Tobagonian. Always will be. It just helps when travelling, or living here. I hope they'll understand that out there. I'll always love Tobago best.'

Well, there could be a bit of flack, when the *Tobago News* finds out. But I'm sure they'll always love you, Dwight ...

Last Word

This book has not been all about football. It's been about a footballer who came from Tobago to Manchester United. All footballers, like all sportsmen, come from nowhere. They don't inherit their place in the team, any team, anywhere, because of something their father did or owned or controlled. You don't find hereditary or even life peers in football. Being a graduate is little help either, as we have seen. Being affable, polite, charming, nice and smiley won't get you a place either, as it can in many professions, though it has to be said that in Dwight's career, those attributes were certainly a plus, remarked on by all who have had dealings with him. They didn't earn him a place when it vitally mattered to him, as Big Ron will testify, but they were certainly a factor when it came to people helping him along the way.

You have to earn it, fight for it, whatever your back-ground, whatever your personality. And then keep fighting for it, whatever you have achieved so far. All pretty normal, really. In that sense, Dwight Yorke's story is normal, has been normal, for the last 100 years since pro football began. A typical working-class story, the rise from nowhere to somewhere. Sir Alex himself went through many of the same hoops. In his day, the cliché was Glasgow or Newcastle, that's where they came from, out of the ship-yards, out of the mines. Now they come from anywhere on the planet.

Dwight's Caribbean background is still relatively unusual in British football. Not many have come from that region. Those with West Indian backgrounds have been mainly second generation, brought up in Britain. John Barnes, who has the charm, social graces, fluency and intelligence of Dwight, came to England very young, attended school here and went on to play for England. So he has to be called a British player, though he does have a faint West Indian lilt. It's remarkable how Dwight's accent is similar, even though he didn't arrive here till he was 17. It's rare in public, even in private, that you are aware of Dwight's West Indian accent. 'Ask' comes out as 'axe' only when he gets excited, or forgets himself.

He is nice, as everyone in this book has said. Never offends, never confronts, never bad tempered, but this does not mean he doesn't get moody, as John Gregory observed, or can't be tough and determined. He is cautious, a rather private person, despite that outward friendliness, doesn't give himself away easily which probably helps to explain the lack so far of a permanent partner in his life. It's also helped to keep him strong, resilient, not swept away, while on his own in a foreign land.

That smile. In a way, it does him a disservice. In photographs, or on television, it tends to distort his face, making his teeth and mouth appear too big for his face. In real life, this doesn't happen. In real life he is much handsomer, much stockier. Now I'm beginning to sound like Sheila. And yes, as you've asked, he does have lovely skin.

While the Caribbean background and laid-back charm are unusual in Britain, being a foreigner isn't. Not today. The Premier League, in England and Scotland, is now filled with them. Taking all our bread, taking all our places, taking all our women, so the critics are now moaning, not giving our British boys a chance. The reply to that is what were our British teams doing all those decades when we had no foreign imports? Not winning many World Cups, is the answer. In fact very often not even qualifying for the World Cup.

What's unusual about Dwight, as a foreigner, is that he signed for Villa as a teenager, not as a mature player, which is mostly the case with our recent star foreign players, such as Klinsmann, Vialli, Zola, who arrived here when in some ways their careers had already peaked.

Dwight, though, tends not to be thought of as a foreigner, having been here so long, rising from the ranks through an English club, coming from an English-speaking country. When you see lists of Best Foreigners, he tends to get forgotten. In lists of Best Buys, he is usually top or very high, which is of course much more flattering, when you think how much was paid for him.

His transfer to Manchester United, the sequence of events and aspirations which motivated it, that will increasingly be a feature of our times. Players have such power these days, whether under contract or not. In Dwight's case, he didn't start it, didn't do it for money, unlike many modern footballers. Our top clubs are very rich today, but they can become impotent when faced with an obdurate player and a tough agent.

Dwight had an agent from a very young age, which was unusual then but not now. He was also lucky that his agent turned out to be one of our leading and most respected ones. The rise and importance of agents, that's another book.

The big piece of luck in his life was Villa coming along when they did. It's hard to fully evaluate, as you can never know what would have happened otherwise. He might have gone to a USA university on a soccer scholarship, as Wendell Moore did, and never been heard of again. Hard to believe that playing for Trinidad and Tobago would not have resulted in some club, from somewhere, coming along. Russell Latapy, who played with Dwight and Lara as schoolboys for Trinidad and Tobago, took a different route – he was spotted by a European not English club and went on to spend five years with Porto in Portugal. (He is now, as I write, in Scotland with Hibernian.)

All players have had similar bits of luck in their careers, in the right place at the right time, but then most of us have, whatever our jobs. We also know you make your own luck, as Dwight certainly did, by hard work and determination to improve.

From now on, while watching Dwight in the flesh or on television, images of Bertille's coaching school will flash into my mind, telling his young charges that SOMEONE HAS TO MAKE IT. I'll also see in my mind's eye Neil Wilson bursting with pride, knowing his US$50 were well spent, and Orville London listening to rather than watching Dwight, checking his fluency and grammar.

Then I'll look at every other player, playing professionally, and know, without knowing the names or contributions, that they are just the same as Dwight. They have a history, they have a background. They might have come from nowhere, but not on their own.